The
Indispensable
Guide to the
Old
Testament

Also in the
Indispensable Guide
Series

The Indispensable Guide to Pastoral Care

by Sharyl B. Peterson

The Indispensable Guide to the Old Testament

Angela Bauer-Levesque

THE
PILGRIM
PRESS
Cleveland

To my students,
past, present, and future

The Pilgrim Press
700 Prospect Avenue
Cleveland, Ohio 44115-1100
thepilgrimpress.com

13 12 11 10 09   5 4 3 2 1

Library of Congress Cataloging-in-Publication Data
Bauer-Levesque, Angela, 1960-
     The indispensable guide to the Old Testament : an introduction /
Angela Bauer-Levesque.
          p. cm.
     Includes bibliographical references.
     ISBN 978-0-8298-1780-5 (alk. paper)
     1. Bible. O.T. – Introductions.   I. Title.
BS1140.3.B38 2009
221.6'1 – dc22

                                                            2008046295

Contents

Preface

With an increasing number of students seeking alternative ways of ministerial training outside traditional M.Div. programs at residential seminaries, eight-week certificate courses have sprung up around the country within the local structures of various Protestant denominations. This text introduces students to basic principles of biblical interpretation and surveys the texts and contexts of the Old Testament/Hebrew Scriptures/First Testament/Hebrew Bible for those interested in progressive theological views (more on the terminology later). Welcome to studying the Bible!

Each week a chapter will guide you through particular sections of your Bible readings, which you will find listed at the beginning of each chapter. At the end of each chapter you will find study questions to help you along. The suggested further readings are to help you pursue some of your new insights in more detail.

Chapter 1 shows you how to move from "ordinary readings" of biblical passages (connecting with the text at face value) to "contextual readings" (bringing the sociohistorical and literary contexts into the conversation) and then still further to "deep readings" (embodying the text as Scripture in particular sociocultural settings to connect with each other). In the process, we survey the types of biblical literature and the most common methods of interpretation.

In chapter 2 we study beginnings. Whether the beginning of a people and nation (Exodus) or the beginning of the cosmos (Genesis), we learn that beginnings involve choices. Introducing the Exodus stories (Exod. 1–15) as the basis for understanding the primeval stories of creation and what follows (Gen. 1–11), the chapter explores the decisions about identity formation of the people of Israel.

Chapter 3 introduces the stories of the covenant making at Sinai and the giving of Torah as foundational moments in the history of the people of Israel. Here we consider the difference between history and story, the latter being about assembling traditions to foster cohesion of a people.

Considering the people's desire to become like everyone else around them, chapter 4 explores the developments toward a monarchy. Based on the Davidic covenant with an individual king instead of the Sinai covenant with the people, the new governing system raises issues of power and perception as witnessed by competing traditions within the Bible.

Then in chapter 5 we learn about the emergence of prophecy, discussing its forms and function vis-à-vis the powers that be. Surveying the organization of the prophetic books, we read stories from the Elijah cycle and the earliest prophetic books of Amos and of Hosea more closely.

Juxtaposing the prophecies of Isaiah of Jerusalem and Micah of Moresheth, chapter 6 shows the similarities and differences of prophetic utterances in Judah as proclaimed from different locations within society. Further, drawing on the prophet Jeremiah's commentary, it traces the history of the people of Israel in the period leading up to the Babylonian exile.

Chapter 7 introduces the prophetic vision of Ezekiel from the rivers of Babylon at the beginning of the Exile, and of Deutero-Isaiah a generation later, exploring messages of hope after the destruction of Jerusalem and the loss of the land. Chapter 8 concludes the book. Here, we listen to various biblical voices (Psalms, Lamentations, Job, Priestly Tradition), noting particularly the richness of their responses to crisis ranging from expressions of lament and mourning to theological reframing of foundational understandings.

No guidebook of this kind is ever written in isolation. From remembering introductions to the Hebrew Bible of my own time as a theology student in Germany and the United States in the 1980s, to recalling the various instances and settings where I have had the privilege to teach such introductory courses myself in seminaries and denominational certificate programs over the past twenty years, I owe thanks to many teachers and students alike: my mentor Luise Schottroff, who was my first teacher of biblical interpretation at the University of Mainz; Eckhart Otto and the late Diethelm Michel, both also in Mainz, and Klaus Koch in Hamburg, whose introductory lectures to the First Testament I attended; my mentor Phyllis Trible at Union Theological Seminary in New York as whose teaching assistant I began my own forays into the field of Hebrew Bible; Norman Gottwald and Richard Weis, who invited me to teach Hebrew Bible at New York Theological Seminary and New Brunswick Theological Seminary, respectively, while I was a doctoral student at Union. Moreover, I continue to be grateful to my students who have kept me honest about

the challenges of interpreting the Hebrew Scriptures, first
at Union, Hartford, Auburn, New Brunswick, and New
York Theological Seminaries, and for the past fifteen years
at Episcopal Divinity School. It is to them, past, present,
and future, that I dedicate this book.

Special thanks go to my former classmate Anne Hoff-
mann, a minister in the United Church of Christ, and my
former students BK Hipsher and Robert Griffin, ministers
in the Metropolitan Community Churches, for continuing
to nag me over the years to write this kind of introductory
text. For special encouragement during the writing process,
I also want to thank Mary Ragan, Alison Cheek, Cristina
García-Alfonso, and Katja Linke.

To bring this guidebook into being, Timothy Staveteig,
publisher of The Pilgrim Press was instrumental. I thank
him for conceiving of this teaching series and inviting me
to consider writing *The Indispensable Guide to the Old Testament*. My editor, Ulrike Guthrie, attended to my every
word with care and sensitivity. Her clarity and affirmation
brought joy to the process, for which I owe her deep gratitude. Likewise, John Eagleson's copyediting and typesetting
merit praise and appreciation. At Pilgrim, I further thank
Joan Blake for shepherding me through the publication
process and making editorial suggestions.

Above all, my spouse, Irma Bauer-Levesque, deserves
unending gratitude as my first and last reader, who caringly
keeps me grounded in reality.

Chapter One

Reading the Bible

From Surface to Depth

Contradictory claims about "the Bible" are nothing new. So let us make one that is deeply true and does not require you to take sides: the Bible is *not* about us; and the Bible is *all* about us. Indeed, throughout history the Bible has functioned in many ways, depending on who has invoked it, in what context, for which purpose. A collection of prose and poetry that was gathered over approximately twelve centuries (ca. 1000 BCE–200 CE) and put together over another twelve (seventh century BCE–fifth century CE), the *Book* contains stories of people of faiths through the ages, struggling with survival, for the most part at the margins of their societies, and struggling with what it means to live as communities of faiths.

So the Bible is not about us — not about Christians or Jews or Muslims or whoever else lives in the twenty-first century CE anywhere. Rather, the Bible is remote in time and place, in language and culture. Given that the earliest materials arose in what we now refer to as the Ancient Near East and became the First Testament with texts written in biblical Hebrew and Aramaic, and that later materials written in Koine Greek were produced and collected in the Roman Empire and became the Second Testament, the cultures and conventions we encounter in the biblical texts present different worlds from our own. Traveling the terrain of the genesis of the Bible, one would have to cover countries on three continents (Asia, Africa, Europe) each with a variety of political circumstances. Given those realities, major challenges arise for translation, as we shall see. Indeed, historically speaking, the Bible is not about us.

At the same time, the Bible is all about us. We see and hear "it" (you may watch and listen and perhaps ask who is referencing what, how, and where for what purpose?) in the daily news and on the Internet. Whether by the children of Hagar and the children of Sarah fighting in Palestine/ Israel over land and water rights, or by the sons and daughters of Ishmael negotiating peace agreements with the sons and daughters of Isaac to end an age-old strife, people of all stripes claim the Bible as a point of reference. We see and hear it claimed in a few particular verses quoted in courts of law to prevent same-sex couples from adopting children or living freely and openly at work or in certain cities and states in the United States. We see and hear the Bible claimed in presidential announcements to try to give credibility to invasions and wars as well as programs and platforms.

Yes, the Bible gets quoted often (far too often in my view) publicly and privately to delineate boundaries, to distinguish between "us" and "them," to self-ascribe religious authority to any in-group by defining itself over against the "other."[1] And I would contend that such practice in itself is problematic, because the Bible becomes merely a collection of proof-texts. For the Bible is not a cookbook full of recipes for life. Neither is it a "how-to" book found in the tech section or the self-help section of your favorite bookstore. I am afraid there are really no recipes (sorry, Ezekiel bread), no shoulds, no blueprints for living in the twenty-first century in our various locations as readers of the Bible. Who really would want to fully re-create the dynamics of the ancient world — food, amenities, rules and regulations, status, and all included?

How else might we use it, you may wonder. For like all engaged readers, we cannot help but read ourselves into the text. The issue is not *that* we do it, but *how* we do it. So how can we make use of it responsibly? How then is the Bible all about us?

1. The Bible is the witness of peoples of faiths through the ages. If we claim to be part of those faith traditions, the Bible is our book.

2. The Bible is a cultural icon in U.S. Christian dominant culture. As participants in this culture, regardless of our position in it, we need to be clear about our relationship to and possible uses of the Bible.

3. The Bible continues to be given authority in churches and synagogues. As participants and leaders in churches we need to find our own ways of claiming the Bible authentically.

4. Biblical references are increasingly claimed to legitimize political decisions in the United States. We need to recognize the power of interpretation and claim *our* interpretations publicly with equal weight.

5. Many theologies of liberation are biblically based, as the Bible has shown a preference for "the least

of these." Thus all those finding themselves at the margins of communities and society have good reason to make use of the liberating powers of the Bible, while being clear (and struggling against) its use to exclude and to legitimize violence against any "others," whenever it occurs.

Thus "the *Book*" has become our Holy Scriptures. We read it, or, to be honest, we read certain parts of it in various translations. Now this guide invites you to read it on multiple levels:

1. There is the reading at face value, "ordinary reading" (as Daniel Patte calls it),[2] the reading that is most widespread and by itself easily in danger of misuse.

2. Then there is the reading that takes into consideration the sociohistorical and literary contexts (it is often called "critical reading" and is still considered in the realm of the theologically educated).

3. Finally, there is what I call "deep reading" (what Vincent Wimbush calls "scripturalizing"),[3] which is the living out of one's scriptural truths in one's particular context/community as a way of living faithfully.

The Bible has been a different book for different people at different times throughout history. Nowadays the Bible contains twenty-four, thirty-nine, or forty-six books depending on whether one picks up a Jewish, Protestant, or Roman Catholic Bible respectively. A Jewish Bible, known as TaNaKh, which stands for the first letters of its three

major sections, Torah, Neviim (Prophets), and Khethu-
vim (Writings), contains twenty-four books. These same
twenty-four books Christians have counted and ordered differently and called the Old Testament with its thirty-nine
books (Samuel becomes 1 Samuel and 2 Samuel; Kings becomes 1 Kings and 2 Kings; etc.). And they have called
these books the Bible when joined with the text they have
called the New Testament. Roman Catholics have added
additional books known as the Apocrypha, while Protes-
tants went back to the thirty-nine books. Since language
of Old and New has had a long history of supersessionism
(meaning that what is new is considered superior to what
is old — though antique dealers would disagree) and thus
has supported anti-Judaism by claiming Christian superior-
ity, some Christians have come to avoid such terminology
and instead talk about First Testament and Second Testament, or Hebrew Bible and New Testament, or Hebrew
Scriptures and Christian Scriptures. None of these terms,
however, is without problems: First and Second introduces
another hierarchy, albeit a historical one; Hebrew Bible
isn't entirely accurate as a description of the First Testament since it includes a few passages in Aramaic; and
Christian Scriptures do include the Hebrew Scriptures as
Scriptures.

In this guidebook we shall refer to the Hebrew Scriptures in the Protestant Bible. They include the Pentateuch,
also known as the Five Books of Moses: Genesis, Exodus,
Leviticus, Numbers, and Deuteronomy. These books con-
stitute what the ancient Israelites and modern-day Jews
have called Torah. The Pentateuch in the Protestant canon
is followed by the Historical Books: Joshua, Judges, Ruth,

1 and 2 Samuel, 1 and 2 Kings, 1 and 2 Chronicles, and Ezra-Nehemiah. In the Jewish Bible some of these books are considered Former Prophets while others belong to the Writings. The Historical Books in the Protestant Bible are followed by Wisdom, consisting of Job, Psalms, Proverbs, Ecclesiastes, and Song of Songs. They are succeeded by the Prophets, the books of Isaiah, Jeremiah, Lamentations, Ezekiel, Daniel, Hosea, Joel, Amos, Obadiah, Jonah, Micah, Nahum, Habakkuk, Zephaniah, Haggai, Zechariah, and Malachi. Of these Lamentations and Daniel belong to the Writings in the Jewish canon.

When most of us open our Bibles, we will read them in translations from the ancient Hebrew, Aramaic, and Greek. Bible translations have had a history almost as old as the Bible itself. To put the Bible in the language of the people, the Hebrew Bible and the Apocrypha were translated into Greek, first in Egypt in the third century BCE. This Greek version is known as the Septuagint because legend has it that seventy or seventy-two scribes were asked to translate it, and according to the Letter of Aristeas (150–100 BCE) all came up with identical translations, a symbolic affirmation of divine inspiration. Until the discovery of the Dead Sea Scrolls in the mid-twentieth century CE, the Septuagint was the earliest witness to the Hebrew Bible; it was *the* Bible of the early Christians as well as the early church until Jerome translated it into Latin, a version that came to be known as the Vulgate, a "Common Language" Bible (completed in 405 CE).

The history of translation of the Hebrew Bible into modern languages has been complicated and contentious. Of the English translations the King James Version, published in 1611, has held a prominent position for close to four hundred years. It is inevitably intertwined with the history of the expansion of the British Empire, a history of colonialism the consequences of which continue to haunt many peoples and places today. While the King James Version (KJV) and the more recent New King James Version (NKJV) are still widely used in the English-speaking and English-reading world, including the United States, for this guidebook we will use the New Revised Standard Version (NRSV), a relatively recent translation by committee, published in 1989. Sponsored and authorized by the National Council of Churches, it is a revision of the Revised Standard Version (RSV) of 1952, and aims at inclusivity in references to humans. The sociopolitical contexts of these and other Bible translations have left their marks on the Bibles we read; and we do well to remind ourselves that all translations are interpretations, which the readers and listeners will in turn interpret further.

The Historical Contexts of the Hebrew Bible

Before we turn to the Hebrew Bible itself, let us put it into its historical contexts. History like story is subject to interpretation, and the history of the biblical world is no different. From whose perspectives are events reported? Where does one begin the story? What is included? Who and what is left out? For example, biblical historians have debated at what point in the history of the biblical world one can claim a resemblance to historical accuracy. While some maintain that nothing historically accurate can be said prior to the Babylonian exile in the sixth century BCE, the time when most of the Pentateuch, the Historical Books, and the Prophetic Books in the Hebrew Bible were gathered together and codified, a majority considers the rise of King David and the beginning of a monarchy in the tenth century BCE as a reliable enough starting point because extrabiblical sources witness to the reported events. The overview below follows the latter and divides biblical history into identifiable premonarchical (before the Davidic monarchy), monarchical (during the Davidic monarchy), and postmonarchical periods (after the fall of the Davidic monarchy). The references are to stories *about* that period rather than *from* that period,[4] as the majority of biblical stories were recorded long after the reported events took place.

Premonarchical

* creation to Babel   [prehistoric]
* stories about the ancestors   [2000–1500 BCE]
* the sojourn and bondage in Egypt   [1700–1290 BCE]
* Exodus   1290 BCE
  (Egyptian records say nothing about
  the Hebrews and the Exodus)
* the time in the desert/wilderness   1290/1250–30 BCE
  including Sinai
* the emergence of Israel in the   1250/1230–1020 BCE
  land, including the time of
  the Judges
* transition to King Saul   1020–1000 BCE

Monarchical

• David=king of Israel and Judah	1000–962 BCE
• Solomon	962–922 BCE
• Northern kingdom/Israel	921–722 BCE
• Southern kingdom/Judah	921–587 BCE

Postmonarchical

• Exile in Babylon	587/586–538 BCE
• Permission to return to the land; beginning of the Persian Empire	538 BCE
• Rededication of the temple: Second Temple period	515 BCE
• Beginning of Hellenization	333 BCE
• Israel's colonial period continued: Ptolemies, Seleucids	223 BCE
• Maccabean revolt	167 BCE
• Hasmonean dynasty	163–63 BCE
• Beginning of the Roman Empire	63 BCE

Archaeologically speaking, the time period covered by the Hebrew Bible coincides mostly with the Iron Age (1200–300 BCE).

Thus, while the Bible is a historical document, it is not historiography — meaning that it does not chronicle events as they happen. Rather, it tells stories about events in the past that have shaped the present; it collects laws and liturgies, sayings and seeds of wisdom. It is a narrative construct, a collection of materials spanning more than a millennium that have been told and retold and thus interpreted since they came into being.

Basics of
Biblical Interpretation

Biblical interpretation, sometimes called "exegesis," from the Greek meaning "to bring out," is as old as the biblical texts themselves. Later passages refer to earlier ones, sometimes reiterating them, other times expanding them or even contradicting them. They do interpret, and so do we. We interpret what we see and hear; we compare the information with what we already know and think; we detect the new and surprising, the strange as well as the familiar, the things that bother us as well as the things that we are comfortable with. There is no such thing as "an innocent eye," or a neutral view. By our upbringing, the contexts we live in, by our convictions and beliefs, by our particular lives we have certain perspectives at any given moment, malleable yet never neutral.

There is nothing wrong with that. What we need to do is to become sensitive to the ways our presuppositions and our social locations influence our reading. This is what *hermeneutics* is about, the exploration of "what" and "how" and "why" we understand, how we make meaning and what meaning we make — trying to be aware what *values* frame our interpretations.

Don't fear. This understanding of the roles of hermeneutics in interpretation is not a free ticket to all interpretations being equally valid or permission to claim anything as biblically based. Neither does it lead to the much dreaded absolute relativism in discussions of postmodernity. Rather, there is always the text in its contexts, in our case the biblical text in context, that stands as a point of departure and return to measure the integrity of the interpretive process.

As a corrective and as a framework for observations on biblical texts, scholars over the last two hundred years have developed several methods that are designed to acquire a better understanding of biblical texts. This list is not complete, and new methodological approaches to the Bible continue being explored — often about ten years after methodologies have arisen in literary, psychological, sociological, and philosophical discourses.

1. We have to find out what text we are dealing with. For readers working with translations this is done by comparing different translations, noting discrepancies or problems with the transmission of the text. The goal of this method is to establish a legitimate text (usually deemed the "original" text). This method is known as *textual criticism*.

2. We have to find out where the text/story begins and where it ends. This is done by reading the literary context of the text/story under consideration and paying attention to the stories before and after. When prior to the eighteenth century CE Moses' authorship was assumed for the Pentateuch, readers observed different versions of the same story (e.g., two creation stories Gen. 1 and Gen. 2; two or three wife-sister stories; Decalogue Exod. 20 and Deut. 5; etc.). They also noticed different names for the deity (YHWH, Elohim, El Shaddai), different writing styles, as well as the inclusion of Moses' death report. All these markers suggest that we are not reading the work

of a single author of a single time and place. A documentary hypothesis (J, E, D, P) was developed (see page 29 below) to determine literary sources behind the text. This method has become known as *source criticism.*

3. We have to find out in what way things are said. It makes a difference for our reading and hearing whether we encounter songs or reports, stories or prayers, commandments or prophecies; etc. As an analogy, consider your reading of the obituary page of the newspaper compared to your reading of the real estate section. Identifying the genre of what we read and thus its functions allows us to understand something about the context of their usage. Many of the genres mentioned are forms used to communicate orally first: stories are told; songs are sung; prophecies are proclaimed; etc. Imagining the social settings of these oral traditions tells us something about the life of the communities who transmitted them. *Form criticism* is the name given to this set of questions or method.

4. Traditions did not come out of nowhere. Older motifs, stories, and myths of Egypt, Mesopotamia, and other areas of the Ancient Near East, transmitted from generation to generation, have left their marks on the biblical stories, as have earlier biblical stories on later ones. So we are invited to compare and contrast as we search for the history of traditions as they move from one setting to another, an approach known as *tradition history.*

5. Having found literary and/or oral traditions, we need
   to account for the composition of the biblical text
   in its present form by suggesting ways it may have
   been put together by later editors. Thus we engage in
   redaction criticism.

6. The final form of the text invites further analysis,
   the study of particularities of a text, its interlocking
   structures thus exposing the art of its composition.
   Such inquiry has been called *rhetorical criticism*, artic-
   ulating form and related meaning as the foundation
   for theological interpretation.

7. Broadening from the particular text to its contexts
   within the wider biblical canon, the method known
   as *canonical criticism* explores theological meanings in
   the way biblical texts work internally within the Bible
   and thus become Scripture.

Other more recent methodologies include *ideological
criticism*, which explores the ideologies of the narrators,
cultural criticism and *postcolonial criticism*, which consider
the ancient and contemporary contexts in terms of power
dynamics within and between texts, cultures, and empires and newer literary methods such as *reader response*
or *deconstruction.*

From this brief survey of some basic methods used in
critical reading of the Bible, you see that there are numerous entry points to exploring biblical texts in their contexts.
While not all of these methods are equally useful for understanding each and every text in the Bible, a combination of
several approaches tends to produce broader insight than
any individual method can by itself. To move from the level

of critical reading to the level of deep reading, it behooves
the reader to ask further questions. I find the following
questions particularly useful:

1. What is life-giving and what is death-dealing in the
    biblical text for any given contemporary context?
2. What power dynamics in the biblical text and context
    relate to ours? and which don't?
3. What alternate biblical voices can be brought into
    the conversation?
4. What and who is benefiting from a particular
    interpretation, and who isn't?
5. What is the conversation, struggle, or issue
    really about?

By seeking answers to these questions, we move deeper into
what matters to us and to our communities about the particular biblical text we encounter. We begin to understand
what it does for us and what it doesn't, and how we want
to use it and for what purpose. Whether in the context
of worship and prayer, or in Bible study and reflection, we
may hear and see the Word anew.

Study Questions

1. What contexts of the Bible can you name? What
    challenges do they pose to your understanding of
    the Bible?
2. What have you learned about the biblical canon?
3. In comparing and contrasting various methods of
    biblical interpretation, what questions arise?

For Further Reading

Tiffany, Frederick C., and Sharon H. Ringe. *Biblical Interpretation: A Roadmap.* Nashville: Abingdon Press, 1996.

Recent Annotated Bibles That Comment on the NRSV

The HarperCollins Study Bible, Fully Revised and Updated. Ed. Harold W. Attridge. San Francisco: HarperCollins, 2006.

The New Interpreter's Study Bible. Ed. Walter J. Harrelson. Nashville: Abingdon Press, 2003.

The New Oxford Annotated Bible with the Apocrypha, Augmented Edition. Ed. Michael D. Coogan et al. New York: Oxford University Press, 2007.

The Peoples' Bible: NRSV. Ed. Curtis P. DeYoung et al. Minneapolis: Augsburg Fortress Press, 2008.

One-Volume Commentaries from Progressive Perspectives

The Africana Bible: Reading Israel's Scriptures from Africa and the African Diaspora. Ed. Hugh R. Page Jr. et al. Minneapolis: Fortress, 2009.

The Global Bible Commentary. Ed. Daniel Patte. Nashville: Abingdon Press, 2004.

The Queer Bible Commentary. Ed. Deryn Guest et al. London: SCM Press, 2006.

The Torah: A Women's Commentary. Ed. Tamara Cohn Eskenazi and Andrea L. Weiss. New York: URJ Press, 2008.

True to Our Native Land: An African American New Testament Commentary. Ed. Brian K. Blount et al. Minneapolis: Fortress Press, 2007.

The Women's Bible Commentary. Ed. Carol A. Newsom and Sharon H. Ringe. Louisville: Westminster John Knox Press, 1992; expanded ed. 1998.

Notes

1. For an excellent study of these dynamics in the Bible, see Lawrence M. Wills, *Not God's People: Insiders and Outsiders in the Biblical World* (Lanham, Md.: Rowman & Littlefield, 2008).

2. Daniel Patte, "Textual Constraints, Ordinary Readings, and Critical Exegeses: An Androcritical Perspective," in *Textual Determinacy: Part One*, ed. Robert C. Culley and Robert B. Robinson, Semeia 62 (Atlanta: Scholars Press, 1993), 59–79.

3. Vincent L. Wimbush, "Reading Darkness, Reading Scriptures," in *African Americans and the Bible: Sacred Texts and Social Textures*, ed. Vincent L. Wimbush (New York: Continuum, 2000), 1–43.

4. Walter Brueggemann, *An Introduction to the Old Testament: The Canon and Christian Imagination* (Louisville: Westminster John Knox Press, 2003).

Chapter Two

Stories of Beginnings

Genesis and Exodus

Read: Genesis 1–11; Exodus 1–18

Whether it is the beginning of a people and nation (Exodus) or the beginning of the cosmos (Genesis), beginnings involve choices and are a matter of interpretation. Where do we find our beginnings, individually and collectively? At birth? At conception? At adolescence? At a time of "coming out" in whatever way we do that? At a time of conversion? Of transformation? At baptism? At initiation? Beginning anew over and over again has characterized not only contemporary times but also biblical ones. You can open your Bible and claim that it begins with the book of Genesis, "When God began to create.../In the beginning, when God created..." (Gen. 1:1). Or you can read the Torah, the Pentateuch, the first section of the Hebrew Bible and notice that the story line of the Hebrew people does not begin before the book of Exodus. Further, you could trace the beginning of these people to the first stories about their ancestors, Abram and Sara and Hagar and their extended clan leaving Ur in Chaldea for the "promised land" (Gen. 12:1–3). Indeed, beginnings involve choices.

It is my choice to introduce the Exodus stories (Exod. 1–15) as the basis for understanding the identity formation of the people of Israel, and the primeval stories from Eden to Babel (Gen. 1–11) as a way our ancestors in faith made sense of their universe later in retrospect.

As we explore the second and the first books of the Pentateuch, we find them a collection of stories from several traditions, woven together at turning points in the history of the people of Israel. While prior to the eighteenth century CE the entire Pentateuch was attributed to Moses — thus the name "the Five Books of Moses" — numerous indicators within these books rule out the possibility of a single author.

For starters, Moses' death is reported (Deut. 34:5). While this might have been explained away as an addendum, duplications and differences in story lines as well as names and theological outlooks suggest a more complex process of biblical composition. For example, the Pentateuch contains two creation stories (Gen. 1:1–2:3 and Gen. 2:4–3:24), two versions of the Decalogue, or giving of the Ten Commandments (Exod. 20:1–17 and Deut. 5:6–21), and other double occurrences (e.g., Gen. 32 and Gen. 35); the story of the flood interweaves different story lines (Gen. 6:19–7:2; see also Gen. 7:12–24), as do others.

Different names for the deity: YHWH (LORD), Elohim (GOD), El Shaddai, El Elyon, etc., point to multiple places and worship traditions (see also Mt. Sinai and Mt. Horeb). So do different theological outlooks, back and forth between a deity portrayed anthropomorphically walking and talking with the people and a god, remote and transcendent, somewhere above. Add to that significant differences in style and vocabulary in the ancient Hebrew, and we realize that the Pentateuch was compiled from different sources over several centuries.

Toward the end of the nineteenth century CE, biblical scholars in Germany, making use of earlier interpretive observations, presented what has become known as the documentary hypothesis.[1] In its classical version it assumes four major literary sources behind the Pentateuch. One is ascribed to a tenth-century BCE writer in the southern kingdom, or Judah (ca. 950 BCE), a particularly vivid storyteller, who stresses the frailty of humankind. Depicting God in anthropomorphic imagery, this author uses the name YHWH for the deity, and thus has been called the Yahwist (J, for *Jahwist* in German). A different theological view of God mediated through messengers, dreams, and visions stresses "the fear of God" in the sense of awe and veneration as foundational for faithfulness. It belongs to a writer in the northern kingdom during the ninth century BCE (ca. 850 BCE), who calls God *'elohim* (prior to Exod. 3:14) and is thus known as the Elohist (E). The primary source of the book of Deuteronomy (especially Deut. 12–26) is called the Deuteronomist (D) and is dated after King Josiah's reform with the "discovery" of the so-called Temple Scroll in 621 BCE (see page 97 below). As we shall learn, Deuteronomy closes the Pentateuch; it also stands at the beginning of the Deuteronomistic History (Deut.–2 Kings). The documentary hypothesis credits the Priestly writer(s) (P) with the final editing and framing of the Pentateuch, after the earlier joining of J and E and the subsequent attaching of D.

P's style tends to monotony, presenting long, detailed lists (e.g., genealogies). Four covenants, from the creation to Noah, from Noah to Abraham, Abraham to Moses/Sinai, and from Moses/Sinai onward delineate the Priestly story line. The divine name YHWH is not used for God before Moses (Exod. 6:2); before this the deity is referred to as El, Elohim, or El Shaddai and depicted as transcendent, lofty, and remote, the Holy One who requires ritual recognition. The Priestly tradition is usually dated during the Babylonian exile (ca. 550 BCE).

Now that we have seen that there were possibly four sources behind the text of the Pentateuch, we wonder how the biblical text we read came into being. The people who wrote all these texts down, all the stories, songs, prayers, etc., certainly did not "invent" all of this; they were not fiction writers. Rather, they were "recorders," listeners to the voices around them, voices of their communities' experiences with their God. Thus we inherit the richness of multiple voices awaiting our interpretations.

Traditionally ascribed to P, Genesis 1:1 starts out, "When God began to create..." and then a little later in Genesis 2:4 we hear J, "In the day that YHWH God made the earth and the heavens...." One beginning, two different beginnings, two versions of one beginning — which is it? To complicate matters, in Exodus 1:8 we read "now a new king arose over Egypt, who did not know Joseph..." — another beginning, this one of the Israelite people. Thus if we choose to begin historically, we should begin with the decisive event that shaped the identity of a people whose struggles and victories the Hebrew Bible witnesses, namely, the Exodus. Yet if we choose to start with the beginning of the book that holds the stories of the people called Israel, we should begin canonically with Genesis. Since without people we wouldn't have stories, I like to begin with Exodus so that we learn about the people first before we read their stories and the ways they made sense of their worlds.

Exodus 1–18

Exodus is the title of the second book of the Bible in the Septuagint, the Greek translation of the third century BCE. It means "the way out" from *hodos* "way" and *ex* "out." In Hebrew, the titles of the biblical books are taken from the first line of the first chapter. For the second book of the Bible it is *shemoth*, "names," from *we'elleh shemoth bene yisrael*, or "these are the names of the children of Israel ..." (Exod. 1:1).

The book of Exodus begins with a series of stories about the Hebrews in the land of Egypt (Exod. 1:8–2:10). Weaving together three traditions, one of the growth of a people, with another about enslavement in Egypt, and yet another about genocide, the story line begins with a historical change, the coming to power of a Pharaoh who had no familiar bond or obligation to this particular group of immigrants (Exod. 1:8). While their strength is useful to the Pharaoh (Exod. 1:9–14), he is threatened by a perceived population explosion of these "foreigners" (Exod. 1:9–10) and orders their enslavement (Exod. 1:11). Nevertheless, the Hebrews' birthrates continue to increase despite the worsening of their enslavement (Exod. 1:12–14). As a supposed stopgap measure, the Pharaoh orders the killing of the enslaved immigrants' male babies (Exod. 1:15–16).

This measure is doomed to failure: according to the story, the midwives refuse to carry out the order because they "feared God" (Exod. 1:17). Their refusal results in a second order by the Pharaoh to drown the baby boys in the Nile instead (Exod. 1:18–22), thus setting up the story that follows (Exod. 2:1–10).

In that story, again women are the ones who defy Pharaoh's orders; they include the mother of a particular baby boy, his sister, and Pharaoh's own daughter. In a dramatic story of crossing lines of class and ethnicity, a Hebrew baby boy is fished out of the Nile River by the Egyptian king's daughter (Exod. 2:5–6), who, mediated by the boy's sister, hires his Hebrew birth mother to nurse the baby (Exod. 2:7–9). Eventually Pharaoh's daughter adopts the boy and names him Moses, a symbolic name meaning "the one drawn out" or "the one drawing out," thus foreshadowing his future role (Exod. 2:10).

Listening to biblical echoes in contemporary contexts, we can hear stories of the borderlands, of immigration and adoption, of crossing lines of ethnicity and class, of lives saved and lives lost.

The biblical story continues, telling about Moses growing up with dual ethnic affiliations and finding himself a *persona non grata* both to the Egyptians and to the Hebrews (Exod. 2:11–15). Thus he flees abroad to Midian; there the refugee meets his future wife, the daughter of a Midianite priest (Exod. 2:16–25).

Then the story shifts to the call of Moses (Exod. 3:1–12). We are told that Moses encountered a messenger of YHWH in a burning bush. In this passage seeing dominates the story before giving way to speaking and hearing:

The messenger of YHWH appeared to Moses in a flame of fire out of a bush; he *looked*, and the bush was blazing but it was not consumed. Then Moses said: "I must turn aside and *look* at this great *sight*, and *see* why the bush is not burned up." When YHWH *saw* that Moses had turned aside to *see*, God called to him out of the bush: "Moses, Moses." (Exod. 3:2–4)

God initiates the theophany, the technical term for a divine appearance, literally "God showing Godself," by calling the name of Moses. God's presence sanctifies the place, that is, making it *qadosh*, or holy, that which is set apart (Exod. 3:4–5). Then YHWH self-identifies as the God of Moses' ancestors (Exod. 3:6) and informs Moses of the divine awareness of the suffering of the enslaved Hebrews in Egypt, calling them "my people" (Exod. 3:7–9). That awareness leads to God's commissioning Moses, therefore "I will send you...," to lead God's people out of Egypt (Exod. 3:10). Divine awareness begets action, which in turn promises liberation.

As typical for call experiences, the one who is being called objects: "Who am I that I should go...?" (Exod. 3:11). And despite being reassured by God and promised a sign (Exod. 3:12), Moses objects again, questioning God's identity (Exod. 3:13). God answers, *'ehyeh 'asher 'ehyeh*, a name giving an identity; an answer that is an attempt not to answer (Exod. 3:14). The Septuagint translates it as *ego eimi ho on*, from which derives the English translation "I am who I am." As the note in the NRSV indicates, the Hebrew is more complicated than that. Suggesting a verbalization of the Hebrew consonants of the divine name *yod-he-waw-he* YHWH, it plays on the verb *hayah* "to be." The Hebrew employs verb forms in what is known in biblical Hebrew grammar as the imperfect tense, which in the forms here suggests incompletion and thus a translation closer to "I will be what I will be."

Puzzled by such meaning, interpreters through the ages have made theological statements from understanding the divine name as the name of the immutable, "I shall be present as I shall be present" (Martin Buber), to reading it as a reference to YHWH as creator, "I cause to be whatever I cause to be" (W. F. Albright).[2] In any case the emphasis is on divine action rather than essence.

Expanding on the notion of the elusiveness of the Divine as well as the fear of consequences for using God's name in vain, Second Temple Jews declared the name of God too holy to appear on human lips and thus refused to pronounce it as written (see below, chapter 8). In reading, they substituted 'adonay — LORD, capitalized — whenever *yod-he-waw-he* appears in the Hebrew text. Consequently the Massoretes, scribes who added vowels to the Hebrew consonants by using a pointing system to give us the text of the Hebrew Bible we use, pointed the Hebrew consonants with the vowels for 'adonay to alert the readers to the need of not reading as written. Unaware of this custom, the monk Petrus Galatinus in the sixteenth century CE transliterated such Hebrew literally as 'Jehovah,' a mistake that is still repeated to this day.

God's self-identification in the Exodus passage continues with God equating YHWH with the God of the ancestors (Exod. 3:15). At this point the Yahwist and the Elohist traditions combine and Moses is commissioned again and given additional assurances (Exod. 3:16–22). Still, Moses

makes objection into an art form, expressing fear of disbelief
(Exod. 4:1) and later inability to speak (Exod. 4:10). He
even pleads for a replacement (Exod. 4:13). Yet eventually
he gives in and returns to Egypt (Exod. 4:18–5:21).

Another revelation of the divine name follows, when
Moses turns to God to complain again (Exod. 5:22–6:13).
Again God self-identifies as YHWH, the God of the ancestors, and this time recalls the shared history of the Sinai
covenant and promises liberation based on this covenant
remembrance (Exod. 6:2–8). Given that such theological
claims jump ahead in the story line, this passage is ascribed
to the Priestly writers.

Now the stage is set for a contest between Pharaoh,
who in Egyptian culture at the time is considered divinity, and Moses, representing YHWH (Exod. 7:1). When
Moses asks Pharaoh to release the Hebrews, Pharaoh refuses, and his heart is hardened (Exod. 7:13). A dramatic
narrative of ten plagues results, throughout repeating the
dynamic of YHWH hardening Pharaoh's heart whenever
he is requested "to let my people go." Throughout, YHWH
is presented as victorious, and eventually the tenth plague
produces the desired result, culminating in the Passover
(Exod. 12) and the crossing of the sea (Exod. 14–15).

Again Yahwist, Elohist, and Priestly traditions are intertwined in presenting a multivoiced record of the Exodus
events. While in J the sea is made into dry land and the
Egyptians drown in the returning waters, in E a messenger of YHWH holds back the Egyptians as the Hebrews
move through. P consequently combines the two, fashion-
ing a third variation about the sea dividing, the Hebrews
moving through, and the sea returning. The fact that these

traditions cannot be harmonized without subordinating one
to another does not diminish the theological importance of
the story, which concludes with a victory song:

> Then Moses and the Israelites sang this song to the
>   LORD:
> "I will sing to the LORD, for he has triumphed
>   gloriously;
> horse and rider he has thrown into the sea.
> The LORD is my strength and my might,
> And he has become my salvation;
> This is my God, and I will praise him,
> My father's God, and I will exalt him.
> The LORD is a warrior;
> The LORD is his name.
> Pharaoh's chariots and his army he cast into the
>   sea. . . . "

Then the prophet Miriam, Aaron's sister, took a tam-
bourine in her hand and all the women went out after
her with tambourines and with dancing. And Miriam sang
to them:

> "Sing to the LORD, for he has triumphed gloriously;
> horse and rider he has thrown into the sea."
>   (Exod. 15:1–21)

While the first verse of the song ascribes it to Moses
(Exod. 15:1), the final verses suggest otherwise (Exod. 15:
20–21). There it is Miriam, identified as a prophet, who is
the leader of the victory song. Indeed, victory songs in the
Bible are frequently associated with women (see Deborah

in Judges 5; Hannah in 1 Samuel 2; Mary in Luke 1:46–55). If this song at the sea had originally been attributed to Moses, nobody would have claimed that it belonged to Miriam. Because it was not, and the people remembered her leadership, we learn about it too. Miriam traditions are retained here, in the book of Numbers, and in the book of Micah, where she is mentioned as one of the triumvirate leading the Exodus, YHWH saying:

> for I brought you up from the land of Egypt,
> and redeemed you from the house of slavery;
> and I sent before you Moses, Aaron, and Miriam.
>
> (Mic. 6:4)[3]

So the Exodus story in the biblical record concludes with a celebration. Historians, however, have wondered about what can really be known historically about the Exodus. What they found is that indeed there is no evidence outside the Bible thus far that the Hebrew people were ever in Egypt. Nevertheless, many records have been found that mention foreigners constantly entering Egypt; and there are Egyptian names in the Bible. In an important collection of documents known as the *Amarna Letters*, constituting official correspondence between some Pharaohs of Egypt and their vassals all over the world, there is mention of a group of people called *'Abiru/Habiru*. They were considered fugitives from their own countries living at the margins of society. You hear similarities to the name "Hebrews" there; and possibly the *Habiru* were some of their ancestors.

During the thirteenth century BCE, during the nineteenth dynasty of the Egyptian Pharaohs, Pharaoh Rameses II (1290–1224 or 1304–1237) came to power. He most likely was the one talked about in Exodus 1:8, even though the Bible does not tell us the name. If that is the case and the reference is to Pharaoh Rameses II, it would allow for enough time for the Israelites to reach Palestine to coincide with the mention of *Israel* as a people on the Merneptah Stele (Pharaoh Merneptah 1224–1211), an upright stone inscribed to commemorate an event or person, the only reference outside the Bible to mention Israel as a people at the time.

In the biblical record, the first half of the book of Exodus presents the Hebrews/Israelites acting as a people with Moses as their primary leader, though traditions of additional leadership by Miriam and Aaron have surfaced. The book continues with a new story of the people on the other side of the Sea of Reeds in the *midbar,* the desert, often translated as "wilderness." There the people enter a time of in-betweens in terms of organization, governance, and theological self-understandings (see page 48 below). Meanwhile, we learn about the people's complaining (Exod. 17), wishing for the "good old times" in Egypt, a human phenomenon of seeing the past through lenses less sharp than those of the present. We also find a story of the origin of YHWH worship among the Midianites (Exod. 18). Eventually, the journey of the people through the desert brings them to Sinai.

The story of the Exodus has been told and retold through the ages. In Judaism it has become the focal point of the annual observation of the festival of Passover, when the story is reenacted in ritual. "How is this night different from all other nights? . . . " (See the Passover Haggadah, the liturgy used during the Passover celebration, which interprets the historical memory of the people.)

In Christian traditions, the Exodus has also figured prominently, from portraying Jesus as the New Moses, to interweaving the Passover with the Passion narrative to various Christian communities identifying themselves as the people of the Exodus for better or for worse. From New England Puritans arriving in the Americas, to enslaved women and men in the antebellum South yearning for an exodus and calling Harriet Tubman a Black Moses, to Boer Nationalists in South Africa identifying themselves with the Israelites and considering the British the Egyptians, questions of "who's really who" abound. Try imagining the Warsaw uprising in the Jewish ghetto taking the Exodus as a model. What happens when a dominant group identifies as the chosen ones? What happens when the group that was oppressed in its original context becomes the oppressor in the new setting?

In recent years, Latin American liberation theologies and black theology have been the most prominent in self-identifying as the Israelites of the Exodus. Both poor peasants and enslaved people of African descent have found empowerment in the story. Critiques have come from womanist theologians,[4] and even more so from First Nation peoples in the Americas,[5] who rather self-identify with Hagar and the Canaanites in the story.

So while we all self-identify with various characters and groups in the biblical texts, it is important to differentiate in order not to use analogies in facile ways. So who are we really?[6]

Back to Genesis

While the book of Exodus has given us the story line of the beginning of the people of Israel, people then as now have wondered about the beginnings of it all, the stories of cosmic beginnings. In the Bible, those stories are collected in Genesis 1–11, also known as the primeval story: five story complexes lead us from creation to the beginning of history. They are (1) the garden story, (2) the story of Cain and Abel, (3) the account of the mixed marriages (between the sons of God and the daughters of humans, (4) the flood, and (5) the story of the tower. All these stories belong to the world of *mythology*, which is to say they are foundational stories of origin offering understandings rather than explanations of human existence.[7] In terms of style, most of the material belongs to the J source, the Yahwist; the rest is ascribed to P, the Priestly writer(s).

Saving a detailed look at Genesis 1 until later during a time of destruction and crisis, when the people need to be reminded of the creation of humankind in God's image, male and female, when they need to be reminded that all creation is good, indeed "very good" (see page 132 below), let us consider the second account of creation more closely now.

The Yahwist, who gave us the creation myth we find in Genesis 2–3, presents it as a myth competing with the dominant myth of his time, namely, the Davidic-Solomonic myth (see chapter 4 below). Over against a presumably glorious kingdom under David and Solomon, the Yahwist stresses the frailty of humankind and holds to the belief that salvation has to come from God.

The garden story has three parts: the development of life (Gen. 2:4b–24), disobedience (Gen. 2:25–3:7), and the disintegration of life (Gen. 3:8–24).[8] Creation begins with YHWH shaping earth/dust and breathing life into it, thus creating the earth creature from the earth:

> Then the LORD God formed the groundling/the
> human/the earth creature
> from the ground/the earth ['adam from 'adamah],
> and breathed into its nostrils the breath of life;
> and the groundling/the human became a living being.
>
> (Gen. 2:7)

Subsequently, God plants a garden, including trees, among them the tree of knowledge of good and evil (Gen. 2:9), of which the earth creature is not to eat (Gen. 2:11). So from the beginning there is a choice. The earth creature is entrusted with tilling and keeping the garden (Gen. 2:15). When the earth creature experiences loneliness, YHWH promises a "helper" as a "partner" (Gen. 2:18). The Hebrew 'ezer kenegdo suggests a right relationship; a relationship that fits, rather than an assistant of lower status. We may want to remember that God is called an 'ezer in the Psalms (see Pss. 33:20; 115:9–11; 121:2; 124:8). Unfortunately, there is a long legacy of reading this verse to suggest that a helper by definition is inferior, thus legitimating misogyny through the ages. Reading what follows closely, we witness the simultaneous creation of woman and man out of the earth creature:

> So the LORD God caused a deep sleep to fall upon
> the groundling/the human/the earth creature,
> and it slept;

then he took one of its ribs and closed up its place
   with flesh.
and the rib that the LORD God had taken from the
   groundling/the human/the earth creature, he
   made into a woman and brought her to the
   groundling/the human/the earth creature.
Then the groundling/the human/the earth creature
   said:
"This at last is bone of my bones and flesh of my
   flesh;
this one shall be called a woman,
for out of a man this one was taken." (Gen. 2:21–23)

So in the juxtaposition of a woman with a man, gender constructions emerge, with the radical notion that the
undifferentiated groundling/human/earth creature was suf-
ficient in itself before. There is even a reversal of traditional
patterns in that the man is moving in with the woman and
her family (Gen. 2:24).

Complicating matters, the serpent appears in the story
and interrogates the woman about the trees in the garden
(Gen. 3:1). The woman responds with her interpretation
of what she heard God say (Gen. 3:2–3). Provokingly, the
serpent juxtaposes his interpretation, including a promise
that eating from the tree will imbue divinity (Gen. 3:4–5).
The story line continues, telling us that the woman eats and
gives some to the man "who was with her" — a line already
left out in the Vulgate by Jerome. Disobedience has entered
Eden; and differences emerge (Gen. 3:7), leading to finger
pointing (Gen. 3:12). When God returns and confronts
the serpent, the woman, and the man, consequences of

disobedience are named (Gen. 3:14–19). The descriptions of a life of hard work and pain in a struggle with harsh nature resemble the realities of the Israelites in the tenth century BCE outside of the royal court. Indeed, they are descriptions, not prescriptions, as is the tragic ending of the story (Gen. 3:23–24).

This latter point we cannot stress enough in light of the misogynistic history of interpretation of the end of the Genesis 2–3 creation story. In other words, just because society in the tenth century BCE ascribed subordinate roles to women, a fact reflected in the Genesis 3 account, responsible biblical theology does not need to uphold gender subordination as God-given. Rather, a careful reading of the story has shown that even in the story itself, the oppressive circumstances are understood as consequence of human disobedience to a divine command.

What follows the story of the garden in the book of Genesis is the story of Cain and Abel, the account of the first murder, the myth of the origin of sin. Note that the word translated "sin" is used for the first time in Genesis 4:7, and not in Genesis 2–3. This is a fact often overlooked throughout the history of interpretation, including in those theological interpretations claiming a concept of "original sin" there. Rather, the biblical narrative locates "sin" for the first time in the destruction of another human being rather than the eating of a forbidden fruit.

The primeval stories also include the story of the mixed marriages, the sons of God having intercourse with the daughters of humans (Gen. 6:1–4). It introduces the flood story (Gen. 6–9), woven together from Yahwist and Priestly sources. Elsewhere in the Ancient Near East other flood stories invite comparisons. Stories of floods have had foundational character through the ages. Here in the book of Genesis the story line moves on to the tower story (Gen. 11:1–9), a description of the challenges of communication and coexistence, a critical Yahwist voice to be sure.

Switching to the memories of the ancestors, the stories in Genesis 12–36 introduce the founding parents of Israel, the three patriarchs (Abraham, Isaac, Jacob) and five matriarchs (Sarah, Hagar, Rebekkah, Leah, Rachel). At a time when the people are already in the land, they recall the promise of progeny (Gen. 12:1–3), the trials and blessings.[9] These ancestor stories explore human relationships amid charting a "family history" of a people. Moving toward the story of the people, the book of Genesis concludes with the long story of Joseph, who functions as the bridge to the book of Exodus, as we saw above (see Exod. 1:8).

Study Questions

1. How do you relate the stories in the book of Genesis to the stories of the book of Exodus 1–18?

2. What have you learned about the divine name YHWH?

3. Comparing and contrasting the Exodus events, what picture emerges of the Exodus?

4. What issues are being raised by the biblical portrayal of the Exodus?

5. How can Genesis 2–3 be read as critique of the reign of David and Solomon?

Further Reading

Dykstra, Laurel. *"Set Them Free": The Other Side of Exodus.*
Maryknoll, N.Y.: Orbis Books, 2002.

Warrior, Robert Allen. "A Native American Perspective:
Canaanites, Cowboys, and Indians." In *Voices from the
Margins: Interpreting the Bible in the Third World,* ed.
R. S. Sugirtharajah, 287–95. 2nd ed. Maryknoll, N.Y.:
Orbis Books, 1995.

Notes

1. Karl Heinrich Graf, 1866; Julius Wellhausen, 1883 (cf.
Jean Astruc, 1753). See, e.g., Anthony Campbell and Mark
O'Brien, *Sources of the Pentateuch* (Minneapolis: Augsburg
Fortress Press, 2000).

2. Martin Buber, *Moses* (reprint Humanity Books, 1988;
orig. 1947); William F. Albright, *From Stone Age to Chris-
tianity,* 2nd ed., with a new introduction (Garden City, N.Y.:
Doubleday, 1919–57; orig. 1940.

3. David Noel Freedman and Frank Moore Cross,
"The Song of Miriam," *Journal of Near Eastern Studies* 14
(1955): 237–50; Phyllis Trible, "Bringing Miriam Out of
the Shadows," *Bible Review* 5 (1989): 14–25, 34.

4. Delores S. Williams, *Sisters in the Wilderness: The
Challenge of Womanist God-Talk* (Maryknoll, N.Y.: Orbis
Books, 1993).

5. Robert Allen Warrior, "A Native American Perspective: Canaanites, Cowboys, and Indians," in *Voices from
the Margins: Interpreting the Bible in the Third World,* ed.

R. S. Sugirtharajah, 2nd ed. (Maryknoll, N.Y.: Orbis Books, 1995), 287–95.

6. Laurel A. Dykstra, *Set Them Free: The Other Side of Exodus* (Maryknoll, N.Y.: Orbis Books, 2002), 50–53.

7. Employing a phenomenological definition, Mircea Eliade in *Myth and Reality* (New York: Harper & Row, 1963) talks about myths as "stories of origins," absolute beginnings (creation) and relative beginnings (institutions).

8. Based on Phyllis Trible, *God and the Rhetoric of Sexuality*, Overtures to Biblical Theology (Philadelphia: Fortress Press, 1978), 72–143; see also *Eve and Adam: Jewish, Christian, and Muslim Readings on Genesis and Gender*, ed. Kristen E. Kvam et al. (Bloomington: Indiana University Press, 1999).

9. Rabbinic tradition: ten trials and seven blessings:

Trials: (1) Leaving home; (2) Dangerous journey to Egypt; (3) Conflict with Lot; (4) Wars with kings from the east; (5) Danger of losing first son; (6) Test of circumcision; (7) Sodom and Gomorrah; (8) Danger to Sarah from Abimelech; (9) Birth of Isaac leading to the expulsion of Ishmael; (10) Binding of Isaac.

Blessings: (1) Gen. 12:1–3; (2) Gen. 12:7; (3) Gen. 13:14–17; (4) Gen. 15; (5) Gen. 17; (6) Gen. 18; (7) Gen. 22:16–18.

Chapter Three

Stories of Foundations
Covenant and the Giving of Torah

Read: Exodus 19–40; read selectively in Leviticus, Numbers, and Deuteronomy

Tracing the memories of the people, we have seen how stories of various families and clans get woven into a story line of a people on their way to becoming a nation. If you find yourself currently in the United States of America, you may want to recall the stories of your own ancestors and how they interweave with the national story: the stories of First Nations peoples on the continent, the creation stories of Big Turtle or Corn Goddess; the stories of various groups of immigrants from Europe and their various claims to the land; the stories of enslaved peoples from Africa and their forced migrations. They/we, too, brought traditions about creation and about floods as well as ancestor stories. The interweaving of these stories continues — sometimes better than others, as those in power tend to dominate the story line. What we find in the book of Exodus is not so different. We have witnessed the stories of liberation and flight from enslavement in Egypt in Exodus 1–18 (see pages 31–39 above).

Exodus 19–40

Now we turn to the second half of the book, where the people forge foundational commitments as a common entity (chapters 19–40). They do that by a religious ceremony binding themselves to their God in a covenant at Mount Sinai, which brings with it agreed-upon rules for communal living.

After several chapters recounting the time "in-between" the Exodus events and the arrival at Mount Sinai, the story continues:

> Israel camped there in front of the mountain. Then Moses went up to God; the LORD called to him from the mountain, saying, "Thus you shall say to the house of Jacob, and tell the Israelites: You have seen what I did to the Egyptians, and how I bore you on eagles' wings and brought you to myself. Now therefore, if you obey my voice and keep my covenant, you shall be my treasured possession out of all the peoples. Indeed, the whole earth is mine, but you shall be for me a priestly kingdom and a holy nation. These are the words that you shall speak to the Israelites." (Exod. 19:2c–6)

Hailed as a pivotal moment in the story of YHWH and the people, YHWH offers the gift of a contract to the Hebrew people (who are called "Israelites" here even though in the story they have not yet entered the land). This contract is called a covenant (*berith*). The covenant at Sinai is a conditional covenant ("if you obey"), based on more ancient international treaties found among the Hittites, an Indo-European people of the kingdom of Mitanni, today's central Anatolia.[1] Similarly structured contracts are called suzerainty treaties because they involve a suzerain/lord and a vassal. Initiated by a superior they offer the inferior protection under the condition of service. The Sinai covenant resembles this dynamic with YHWH as the initiator and the people as the ones promising obedience in exchange for covenantal privileges. Thus it is unlike the covenant God made with Abraham (Gen. 15), which was unconditional. Based in the history of any preceding relations ("you have seen what I did..."), it spells out obligations ("if you obey...") and contingent rewards ("you shall be..."). Drawing on political treaties theologically, the Sinai covenant establishes a special nation called to the privilege of a special relationship with YHWH: "a kingdom of priests" under God, the king; "a holy nation." Moses takes the offer back to the people, and the people "choose" to do it:

> The people all answered as one: "Everything that the LORD has spoken we will do." (Exod. 19:8)

Upon their agreement, the people are consecrated, which means they are declared special in the eyes of God, set apart from other peoples. Keep in mind that we are reading this in a report written from the perspective of those who benefit from this arrangement.

If being declared a holy nation was not enough, the people are offered another gift, the gift of Torah. The Hebrew word *torah* is often translated into English as "law" and then unfortunately juxtaposed to the "gospel," the "good news," which by dualistic implication suggests that this "law" is the opposite or at least less than. The long history of Christian anti-Judaism and related anti-Semitic violence witnesses to the danger of such perception. Thus we, today's readers, are obliged to become aware of these dynamics and try to stop them wherever we can.

A more accurate translation of *torah* is "instruction." Such instruction can be found in several sections of the Hebrew Bible, especially the Covenant Code (Exod. 20–23), the Holiness Code (Lev. 17–26), and the Deuteronomic Code (Deut. 12–26). Among the legal instructions of the Hebrew Bible, the Decalogue (or Ten Commandments) is the best known.[2] It is found in a couple of versions, in Exodus 20:1–17 and Deuteronomy 5:6–21, and in ritual terms in Exodus 34:10–28.

In the Decalogue, as you probably know, most commands are stated in the negative: "you shall not . . . ," thus allowing for a greater freedom in what is not said than a positive order would. Exodus 20:1–17 begins with the command of faithfulness to YHWH alone, followed by instructions on how to worship this god:

> I am the LORD your God, who brought you out of the land of Egypt, out of the house of slavery; you shall have no other gods before me. You shall not make for yourself an idol, whether in the form of anything that is in heaven above, or that is on the earth beneath or that is in the water under the earth. You shall not bow down to them or worship them; for I the LORD your God am a jealous God, punishing children for the iniquity of parents, to the third and the fourth generation of whose who reject me, but showing steadfast love to the thousandth generation of those who love me and keep my commandments. (Exod. 20:2–6)

After a historical introduction, remembering what God has already done for the people, there comes a prohibition against divine images. It is rooted in the theological understanding that humans themselves are the created image of God (see Gen. 1:26–27), and that God walks among them and with them, rather than being "captured" somewhere to be visited.

> You shall not make wrongful use of the name of the LORD your God, for the LORD will not acquit anyone who misuses his name. (Exod. 20:7)

Based in the understanding that name and person are identical, the command to not swear falsely by the divine name constitutes a prohibition against perjury, where God's name would be misused under oath.

This string of negative commands is followed by a detailed positive command to keep the Sabbath as the day that completes creation:

> Remember the sabbath day, and keep it holy. Six days you shall labor and do all your work. But the seventh day is a sabbath to the LORD your God; you shall not do any work — you, your son or your daughter, your male or female slave, your livestock, or the alien resident in your towns. For in six days the LORD made heaven and earth, the sea, and all that is in them, but rested the seventh day; therefore the LORD blessed the sabbath day and consecrated it. (Exod. 20:8–11)

Having ordered the relationship between God and the people, the instructions turn to address the relationships among the people flowing from such divine-human connection.

> Honor your father and your mother, so that your days may be long in the land that the LORD your God is giving you.
> You shall not murder/kill.
> You shall not commit adultery.
> You shall not steal.
> You shall not bear false witness against your neighbor.
> You shall not covet your neighbor's house; you shall not covet your neighbor's wife, or male or female slave, or ox, or donkey, or anything that belongs to your neighbor. (Exod. 20:12–17)

Healthy community living depends on care and respect for the elders (Exod. 20:12), on respect for each other's life (Exod. 20:13) and for each other's possessions (Exod. 20:14–15), just as lack of respect for these leads to unrest and violence against each other. The command not to take someone's life has been translated into English variously as either "you shall not murder" (preferred by those in favor of the death penalty) or "you shall not kill" (preferred by its opponents). The Covenant Code very much claims the latter as it specifies different penalties for those who kill intentionally and those who kill accidentally. In the United States as in most countries, criminal law to this day upholds these distinctions. Please also note that adultery is included in this litany of possible offenses because contrary to contemporary understandings of human rights, adultery at the time was considered primarily an offense against another man's property. Further, protection is needed for a man's social honor (Exod. 20:16) as well as safety from constant emotional threats to his property (Exod. 20:17).

As you see from the absence of women both in audience and in content, not all members of the community are treated equally. Thus it is important to remember that invoking the Ten Commandments today as contemporary rules for living intentionally or unintentionally reimports those social dynamics.

According to the book of Exodus, the parameters for community living laid out in the Ten Commandments are witnessed by nature through thunder and lightning, by trumpet sound and mountain smoke, just as the treaties of the Hittites were (Exod. 20:18). What follows in the so-called Covenant Code are detailed instructions containing some of the oldest legal material in Scripture. They spell out the particularities of life as a covenant people, with guidelines for worship and rules about possessions, including rules governing their acquisition, loss, or exchange. Again, the historical context is one of patriarchal ownership (Exod. 20:22–23:19).

The giving of Torah ends with the promise of the conquest of Canaan (Exod. 23:20–33) and is followed by a covenant ceremony, where the covenant is accepted:

> Moses came and told the people all the words of the LORD and all the ordinances; and all the people answered with one voice, and said, "All the words that the LORD has spoken we will do." (Exod. 24:3)

In a ceremony the covenant is sealed in blood (Exod. 24:4–8). Following the ceremony, the people are asked to build a sanctuary ("have them make a sanctuary so that I may dwell among them" [25:8]) and to construct the tabernacle containing the ark of the covenant, which is described in detail in the following chapters (Exod. 25–31). The story continues with the making of the ark, a portable shrine made of acacia wood, containing the tablets and symbolizing the presence of God, invisibly constituting a throne for YHWH. Thus the ark becomes a portable Sinai, a place that transcends any particular location.

While most of the materials of the making of the covenant at Sinai and the Covenant Code are attributed to northern traditions (E), most of the instructions on the making of the tabernacle are considered Priestly material (P). In the southern traditions (J) there is yet another symbol, the "tent of meeting" (Exod. 32–34).

In the book of Exodus all three traditions coexist, providing a richly layered presentation of what has become a central tenet of Hebrew faith. Sharing the understanding of the conditionality and the binding character of the Sinai covenant, both northern and southern traditions hold it as a symbol that offers an identity to a people, known as a "mixed multitude" (see Exod. 12:38). The emerging differences between North and South regard the role of the people and issues of leadership. While the North maintains the participation of all the people in witnessing the theophany as well as the social character of the Torah, the South emphasizes Moses' leadership as covenant mediator with the people as recipient witnesses to instructions regarding religious rituals. The restatement of the commandments in Exodus 34:6–26 shows this clearly. They are much more detailed than Exodus 20:1–17 and focus on worship and ritual.

Both traditions were joined in the retelling of how the people remembered the Sinai events. Later during the time of the Babylonian exile in the mid-sixth century BCE, they were framed by Priestly editors in the final composition of Torah.

Leviticus and Numbers

Following the book of Exodus, the book of Leviticus is a collection of legal material ascribed to the Priestly source, different in style from Genesis and Exodus (narratives). Its major theme is purity, universally portrayed by the preservation of cosmic harmony in nature and society as well as individually by the attention to personal holiness and honor. In Christian traditions Leviticus has become associated with dietary laws and instructions on sexual relations, social ethics, and ritual that most Christians have chosen to ignore, or worse, to apply selectively to all those considered "other" for the purposes of exclusion.[3] I am thinking here especially of Levitical passages quoted against women, against Jewish people, or more recently against LGBT people. We may want to remember that amid these passages of the Holiness Code (Lev. 17–26) we find the command "you shall love your neighbor as yourself" (Lev. 19:18b). It is this command that later on Jesus of Nazareth is credited with calling the greatest combined with Deuteronomy 6:5, "you shall love the LORD your God with all your heart, and with all your soul/being, and with all your might" (Matt. 22:34–40).

In the First Testament after the book of Leviticus, the story line of the book of Exodus continues in the book of

Numbers. By comparison Numbers appears rather disorganized, as the story line is frequently interrupted by pieces of religious instruction and legal materials. Describing first the organization of the Hebrew people before their departure from Sinai (Num. 1:1–10:10), the book moves on to tell of their travels through the *midbar*, the mostly rocky desert from Sinai to the Plains of Moab. It continues with stories about the preparation for entry into "the land." Along the way it introduces its readers to leadership struggles and issues of authority between Moses and his siblings Aaron and Miriam (e.g., Num. 12 and 20), and intergenerational squabbles between those who had suffered in Egypt and those who had grown up thereafter. Tensions surface during a time of unsettledness. Likewise, unresolved issues concerning such matters as inheritance require solutions, as the daughters of Zelophehad can attest (Num. 27 and 36), when traditional patriarchal lines are crossed.

In terms of canonical biblical literature, the book of Deuteronomy follows. It functions as the hinge that enables the transition from the Pentateuch to the Former Prophets. As the fifth book of Torah, Deuteronomy brings Torah to a close. In terms of writing style and theological views, Deuteronomy has more in common with what has become known as the Deuteronomistic History (Joshua through 2 Kings).

Major parts of the book of Deuteronomy are said to be discovered during King Josiah's reform and the temple renovation that was part of it in 621 BCE. We shall return to it in detail in chapter 6 when we have traveled with the people of Israel to that point.

Study Questions

1. How do you relate the stories in the second half of the book of Exodus (Exod. 19–40) to the stories in the first half (Exod. 1–18)?
2. What have you learned about the covenant at Sinai?
3. How does this covenant compare to earlier treaties? How does it compare to other biblical covenants?
4. What issues are being raised by the translations of the Hebrew *torah*?
5. How do you understand the Holiness Code compared to the Covenant Code?

Further Reading

Brenner, Athalya, ed. *Exodus to Deuteronomy: A Feminist Companion to the Bible.* Second series, no. 5. Sheffield: Sheffield Academic Press, 2000.

Plaskow, Judith. *Standing Again at Sinai: Judaism from a Feminist Perspective.* San Francisco: Harper & Row, 1990.

Notes

1. George Mendenhall, *The Tenth Generation: The Origins of the Biblical Tradition* (Baltimore: Johns Hopkins University Press, 1974).

2. For in-depth interpretations of each commandment, see Walter Harrelson, *The Ten Commandments and Human Rights*, Overtures to Biblical Theology (Philadelphia: Fortress Press, 1980).

3. See Alan Cooper and Susanne Scholz, "Leviticus," in *Global Bible Commentary,* ed. Daniel Patte (Nashville: Abingdon Press, 2004), 30–42, for an example of a constructive and respectful dialogue commenting on these passages.

Chapter Four

From Movement to Institutions

David and Solomon

Read: Joshua and Judges selectively; 1 Samuel 1–12, 15, 28; 2 Samuel 1–2, 5–7, 9–20; 1 Kings 1–2, 12; reread Genesis 2–3

In the story of the Hebrew people, we have read and heard the story of their liberation, the story of the Exodus, the story of their deliverance from enslavement, and we have skimmed the story of their time in the wilderness. According to the story line, after forty years in the wilderness, the people settle in the land (*'eretz*). The stories of this "settlement" in the land are recorded in the book of Joshua and the beginning of the book of Judges.

Moving from the Pentateuch to the Historical Books, we become aware of a shift in writing style and perspectives. The books of Joshua and Judges are part of the so-called Deuteronomistic History,[1] a "history" modeled on the theology of the book of Deuteronomy. I put "history" in quotation marks because our contemporary understandings of historiography, the ways we record history in the twenty-first century CE, are much more concerned with chronology and data collection than was the case in Ancient Israel. There, the story line takes precedence. In

their present form, the biblical books of Joshua through
2 Kings portray the (hi)story of Israel from the Mosaic period into the Babylonian exile, written from a perspective of
divine retribution against the whole people of Israel. This
represents an editing of earlier sources by an individual
who lived during the exile in the sixth century BCE, trying in general to explain how it happened that the Davidic
dynasty came to an end despite the promises of an eternal
kingdom in 2 Samuel 7.

The commonly known story line continues according to
the book of Joshua. By the end of the book of Deuteronomy, the people have arrived at the "promised land." We
note that so far the theme has been *land giving, not land taking,* the promise of a land chosen for Israel, not chosen by
Israel, a land that is not a possession but contingent upon
obedience to the covenant. That is going to change in the
Joshua narrative, where conquest is the dominant theme.

Through the ages some biblical scholars have wondered
what can be known about Israel's emergence in the land.
According to the Egyptian inscription of Merneptah (see
page 38 above), some sort of ethnic entity called "Israel"
must have existed shortly before 1200 BCE. How is this
"Israel" related to the Israel we read about in the Hebrew
Scriptures?

Based primarily on the first half of the book of Joshua
(Josh. 1–12) and supporting archaeological evidence of
destroyed cities, some U.S.-based scholars in the mid-
twentieth century championed a conquest model.[2] They
assumed a concerted effort by all of Israel united under
one leader named Joshua to make a sudden, bloody, complete conquest of the land west of the Jordan, taking the

land in three successive campaigns. Where this model falls
short is in making sense of contradictions within both biblical and archaeological sources. For example, within the
book of Joshua and between the books of Joshua and Judges
some peoples, who are said to be wiped out completely, appear a few chapters later alive and well, fighting once again
(e.g., Josh. 10:33 vs. 16:10 regarding the people of Gezer;
Josh. 10:38–39 vs. 15:15 regarding Debir; or Josh. 10:42
vs. 11:18 vs. 13:2–3 regarding Gaza; or the beginning of
Judges 1 compared to Josh. 11:16–20). Further, findings
of archaeology raise questions about the historicity of the
Joshua narrative. For example, the excavation of Jericho
showed it as an ancient city dating back to the eighth
millennium BCE, while raising doubts about whether it
was settled at all in the thirteenth century BCE. Similarly,
archaeological evidence shows that the city of Ai was un-
inhabited from 2200 to 1000 BCE. Other cities did show
thirteenth-century BCE destruction (e.g., Lachish, Eglon,
Debir, Bethel, Hazor).

Partly in response to this conquest model, some German
scholars after World War II put forth an alternative model
of peaceful infiltration and gradual settlement as the way to
understand Israel emerging in the land of Canaan.[3] Based
on the book of Judges and the fact of the above-mentioned
discrepancies in the book of Joshua, they imagined a complicated process of infiltration and amalgamation with the
indigenous inhabitants of the land, suggesting that the
Hebrew people were semi-nomads, moving their livestock
according to pasture and season, gradually staying on and
settling down, at first in parts of the Judean hill country. They accounted for the destruction of some cities at

the time by attributing it to wars between Canaanite city-states. Where that model falls short is in accounting for the destruction of particular Canaanite cities as well as the assumption of Bedouin patterns not attested to in that location.

Steeped in sociological observations and dissatisfied with the two earlier models, some U.S. biblical scholars in the 1960s and 1970s challenged the assumption of shepherds turned farmers and proposed a third model — an internal Canaanite peasant revolt against the cities.[4] They suggested that an uprising of peasants against the city-states was catalyzed by a group of marginalized outsiders, known as 'Abiru/Habiru, who had escaped from Egypt, and were bound together by a covenant allegiance to their God YHWH. Further, this model assumes that this core group from Egypt rejected Canaanite religious and social practices and strove for a redistribution of power and resources toward a more egalitarian design via an "internal conquest." Chapters 12 and 24 in the book of Joshua and some sections in the book of Judges provide the biblical base for this model. Archaeological evidence of settlement patterns and the Byblos correspondence in the Amarna letters (see page 37 above) regarding the 'Abiru/Habiru serve as extra-biblical sources. The dominant story line in the book of Joshua of a complete conquest is considered to be the work of a later historian who needed to legitimize the status quo of the time. Discrepancies in sociological and archaeological data have hampered the arguments of this model. Since then, models that combine various strands of settlement data and ideological critique of the biblical sources have emerged.[5]

What this brief survey of models for understanding the emergence of Israel in the land shows is that the biblical stories suggest contradictory realities, complicated by archaeological evidence and insights from sociological research. What we can say with certainty are three things: namely, that at the time (ca. 1200 BCE) there was a population increase in the area that is not explicable on the basis of natural causes; that settlement patterns were shifting; and that within biblical stories an Israelite identity was developing linked both to the Sinai covenant and to "the (promised) land."

According to the biblical sources, the Israelites were in a boundary period between the childhood and the adulthood of a people, between the great leaders Moses and Joshua and the coming of the monarchy with David and Solomon, between movement and institution.

In terms of identity formation, we find the conflation of traditions in that the new leader, Joshua, is portrayed like a copy of Moses: both are said to have sent spies; both are said to have led crossings of the sea/river; both have ceremonies of circumcision to precede Passover (Exod. 12/ Josh. 5); both are recipients of a theophany with the same words: "take off your shoes . . ." (Exod. 3/Josh 5); both receive the law at a mountain (Moses at Mt. Sinai/Joshua at Mt. Ebal); and both function as covenant mediators (Exod. 19/Josh. 24). What distinguishes the two is what we do not learn about Joshua: any of his doubts and struggles. Rather, the portrayal of Joshua is monodimensional. This suggests later editorial enlargement of a historical Ephraimite leader into an ideal leader of all the Israelites. The covenant making/restating at Shechem provides a wonderful example of the weaving of traditions to include those who had been in Egypt, those who joined in the *midbar*, those who never left the land of Canaan, and others who were in attendance (Josh. 24). Canonically, the book of Judges continues the story line of Joshua, yet it contradicts its content in numerous places. At its core we find a collection of stories about leaders/judges who are portrayed as saviors of the people after the previous leader and the people have failed. Covering the Iron Age years of 1200–1050 BCE, the savior stories follow a fourfold scheme of apostasy (Israel sins by turning away from YHWH), invasion (Israel is conquered as punishment), repentance (Israel realizes its sin and turns around), and deliverance (YHWH intervenes and delivers Israel through a new judge).

Rather than being legal professionals, these judges were military leaders with charismatic gifts, which they claimed came from the spirit of YHWH. Portrayed as living in liminal times, individual judges such as Deborah or Gideon stand out in how they are remembered at the thresholds of political and social boundaries. Women play a significant role throughout the book, as the boundaries between public and private spheres appear not yet clearly established (see Achsah, Judg. 1:12–15). Among them are daughters of Israel and daughters of the foreigners (3:6), Deborah (4–5), Jael (4–5), the mother of Sisera (5:28–30), the concubine of Gideon/the mother of Abimelech (8:31–9:1), the woman with the millstone (9:52–57), the mother of Jephthah (11:1), the daughter of Jephthah (11:29–40), daughters of Israel (11:40), daughters of Ibzan (12:8), the wife of Manoah/the mother of Samson (13:2–24; 14:1–7), the daughter of the Philistines (14:1–15:6), the harlot of Samson (16:1–3), Delilah (16:4–22), the mother of Micah (17:1–4), the woman/concubine of Bethlehem (19:1–30), the virgin daughter (19:24), the virgins of Jabesh-Gilead (21:10–12), and the daughters of Shiloh (21:23).

Overall, the book of Judges is framed by the Deuteronomistic editors to raise the question of how Israel could live without a great leader, suggesting that it did live through those times but not always well. Thus, by the end of the book of Judges, the Deuteronomistic Historian calls for a king.

Threatened from within and from without, Israel sought a change in its way of life: a king, to become like the Canaanites and to meet the threat of the Philistines. While the threat of the Canaanites was internal, the threat of the Philistines was an external one — and therefore also a military threat. The Philistines, an Indo-European people also known as the "sea peoples," invaded Egypt in the twelfth century BCE. Later they were driven out and moved north into Canaan, where they settled on the south coast. A military aristocracy, they built a system of five city-states (Gaza, Gath, Ashkelon, Ashdod, Ekron). They had a monopoly on iron, a precious metal at the time, and they developed the military strategy of chariot battles. They were also known as brewers of beer (*shekar*: typically translated as strong drink).

Internally, the people's desire for a king contradicted the tenets of the Sinai covenant, where YHWH alone is the invisible king of a kingdom of priests (Exod. 19:6). We see this tension in the relationship of Saul of Benjamin, who became the first king, and Nathan the prophet representing Samuel; as a pair, they stood for the two poles, pro- and

anti-monarchy. We find both intertwined in the books of
Samuel (1 Sam. 8:4–22).

Samuel, dedicated at birth to become a Nazirite, grew up
at the shrine of Shiloh as a protégé of Eli. He represents the
"intolerance of YHWH faith" and is said to have made no
accommodation for Canaanite religious practices. Ambigu-
ity marked his attitude toward the monarchy, yet he was
unable to meet the Philistine threat (1 Sam. 9:15–10:1).
By contrast, Saul was a military leader with great charismatic gifts, who even as a king would be more like the
judges. Samuel anointed and opposed Saul; he sheltered
David when David fled from Saul (1 Sam. 19).

After Saul's death, David was made king over the house
of Judah. Invited by the people of Israel (2 Sam. 5:1–3),
David also became king over Israel, thus placing two kingdoms under one king. This so-called "United Monarchy"
constituted a personal rather than a political union that
would last for just two generations.

David succeeded in subduing the Philistines and became king of the Philistines. He also became king of the
Jebusites when he decided that he needed another capital, choosing the ancient city and national fortification of
Jerusalem. Jerusalem thus became the political center of
David's realm. To make it also the religious center, David
moved the ark there, after retrieving it from obscurity.
The idea of making the ark stationary constituted a radical
break with Sinai tradition. It was another step toward turning a movement into an institution. Nevertheless, under
King David the ark resided in a tent in Jerusalem.

Theologically, these moves are legitimated with the
story of the making of a covenant between YHWH and

David, made unconditionally and promised to last forever (2 Sam. 7). Simulating God's covenant with Abraham
(Gen. 15), it is presented as the fulfillment of the promises
to Abraham (Gen. 12:1–3) and serves as an authentication
of David and a Davidic dynasty.

Your house and your kingdom shall be made sure
forever before me; your throne shall be established
forever. (2 Sam. 7:16)

And you established your people Israel for yourself to
be your people forever; and you, O LORD, became
their God. And now, O LORD God, as for the word
that you have spoken concerning your servant and
concerning his house, confirm it forever; do as you
have promised. Thus your name will be magnified forever in the saying, "The LORD of hosts is God over
Israel"; and the house of your servant David will be
established before you. For you, O LORD of hosts, the
God of Israel, have made this revelation to your servant, saying, "I will build you a house"; therefore your
servant has found courage to pray this prayer to you.
And now, O Lord GOD, you are God, and your words
are true, and you have promised this good thing to
your servant; now therefore may it please you to bless
the house of your servant, so that it may continue forever before you; for you, O Lord GOD, have spoken,
and with your blessing shall the house of your servant
be blessed forever. (2 Sam. 7:24–29)

With the overwhelming stress on the Davidic line lasting
forever, the Deuteronomic historians make a point about

the stability of the new institution. Yet not all are so positive about the new monarchy and its monarch.

While in these royal victory traditions we see a strong David, the Succession Narrative (2 Sam. 9–20; 1 Kings 1–2)[6] exposes us also to anti-Davidic propaganda: as a father and family leader, David is a failure (see especially 2 Sam. 11–13). Political intrigue dominates the remainder of 2 Samuel with one after another of possible successors killed, until eventually Solomon secures the throne and is anointed by his father David (1 Kings 2:1–4) shortly before David's death.

Over time King David has become a symbol. In the Bible he is treated as the norm of the ideal king (". . . walking in the footsteps of David"); as a prototype of the messiah ("the anointed one"); as inspiration for the liturgical literature of Israel (many psalms are ascribed to him); and as the founder of a theology and religious practices centering in Zion/Jerusalem.

David's son Solomon then becomes the second emperor. He openly lets his enemies be killed; he is a master of business deals, e.g., with the queen of Sheba, which leads to the control of the caravan trail and gives Israel a harbor; he introduces forced labor and heavy taxation; he is the king of the building boom, including many buildings in the city of Jerusalem and the most ambitious project, the temple (1 Kings 5–8). By imposing administrative and economic control over the land, Solomon makes Jerusalem not only politically but also symbolically the center of the cosmos. He is remembered as a great diplomat and rhetorician, as well as a king of wisdom (see 1 Kings 3; 4:29–34).

Tradition has ascribed to Solomon three major wisdom books: Proverbs, Song of Songs, and Qoheleth/Ecclesiastes. It is in the time of Solomon that the Yahwist writes. So contrast the opulence and grandeur of the monarchy in the tenth century BCE with the creation of human beings from dust. Genesis 2–3 read against this backdrop counters the excesses of the monarchy (see page 40 above).

Soon others, too, perceive problems of such an idyllic royal construction. After Solomon's death it becomes obvious that the kingdom has had problems from its inception (1 Kings 12:1–20). Fueled by heavy taxation, discontent leads to rebellion, resulting in the breakaway of the northern kingdom, Israel, in 922 BCE. While the immediate causes are seen in the policies of Solomon's successor Rehoboam, deeply engrained differences between Israel and Judah socially and economically as well as resentment about the centralization of religious observances in Jerusalem support the division. A fragile union breaks apart again, with Israel going its separate way.

With this division a new religious phenomenon emerges where two independent kingdoms are worshiping the same god, YHWH. In the North, King Jeroboam returns from exile in Egypt and makes Shechem, the established religious center for the North, his capital. His reign lasts for about twenty-one years, and he is succeeded by his son, Nadab, who reigns for less than a year before he is assassinated by Baasha, who then reigns for twenty-three years. Baasha is followed by his son Elah, who lasts for about a year before he is assassinated by Zimri, who lasts one week and possibly committed suicide.

Next, King Omri (876–869 BCE) succeeds in establishing a dynasty of some four generations (885–843 BCE) until the rise of Jehu. Omri entered into a close alliance with the southern kingdom/Judah, assuring peace and a time of prosperity for the northern kingdom while acquiring international fame ("the house of Omri"). He married his son off to a Phoenician princess. He is the first individual in Hebrew history to be mentioned in extrabiblical material, the so-called Mesha stele of the records of Assyrian ruler Shalmanezer III; yet the Bible devotes no more than thirteen lines to him. The Deuteronomistic historians condemn him as a Baal worshiper while they say nothing about his tribal background nor anything about his achievements; they resent his alliance with Ithobaal, the king of Phoenicia.

King Ahab (873–851 BCE) marries the Phoenician princess Jezebel, who becomes queen of the Israelite empire. As a worshiper of Baal Melkart she wants to spread her faith, requiring an official position for her religion along with Yahwism. Her husband, Ahab, participated in this religion and is said to have built a temple for Baal (1 Kings 16). But Baalism and Yahwism are incompatible, as Jezebel well understands. And so does Elijah, whom we shall meet in the next chapter.

Study Questions

1. How do you understand the formation of the people of Israel?

2. What have you learned about various models for Israel's emergence in the land of Canaan?

3. What are the strengths and the weaknesses of these models?

4. How do you make sense of the book of Joshua compared to the book of Judges?

5. What are some of the characteristics of the Deuteronomistic History (content, composition, historical contexts, etc.)?

Further Reading

Pixley, Jorge V. *Biblical Israel: A People's History* Minneapolis: Fortress Press, 1993.
Levenson, Jon D. *Sinai and Zion: An Entry into the Jewish Bible*. San Francisco: Harper & Row, 1985.

Notes

1. Martin Noth, *The Deuteronomistic History* (Sheffield: Sheffield Academic Press, 1981; orig. 1943); Frank Moore Cross, *Canaanite Myth and Hebrew Epic: Essays in the History of the Religion of Israel* (Cambridge, Mass.: Harvard University Press, 1973).

2. William F. Albright, "Archaeology and the Date of the Hebrew Conquest of Palestine," *Bulletin of the American Schools of Oriental Research (BASOR)* 58 (1935): 10–18; also "The Israelite Conquest of Canaan in the Light of Archaeology," *BASOR* 74 (1939): 11–23; John Bright, *A History of Israel*, 3rd ed. (London: SCM, 1981); George E. Wright, *Biblical Archaeology*, 2d ed. (Philadelphia: Westminster Press, 1962).

3. Albrecht Alt, "The Settlement of the Israelites in Palestine," in *Essays on Old Testament History and Religion* (Oxford: Blackwell, 1966; orig. 1948); Martin Noth, *The History of Israel* (London: Blackwell, 1960; orig. 1957); Gerhard von Rad, *The Problem of the Hexateuch and Other Essays* (Edinburgh: Oliver & Boyd, 1966; orig. 1958).

4. George E. Mendenhall, "The Hebrew Conquest of Palestine," *Biblical Archaeologist* 25 (1962): 66–87; Norman K. Gottwald, *The Tribes of Yahweh: A Sociology of the Religion of Liberated Israel, 1250–1050 BCE* (Maryknoll, N.Y.: Orbis Books, 1979).

5. Manfred Weippert, *The Settlement of Israelite Tribes in Palestine* (London: SCM, 1971); Robert B. Coote and Keith W. Whitelam, *The Emergence of Early Israel in Historical Perspective*, Social World of Biblical Antiquity Series 5 (Sheffield: Almond Press, 1987); Niels Peter Lemche, *Ancient Israel: A New History of Israelite Society*, Biblical Seminar 5 (Sheffield: JSOT Press, 1988); Baruch Halpern, *The Emergence of Israel in Canaan* (Chico, Calif.: Scholars Press, 1983).

6. Leonhard Rost, *The Succession to the Throne of David* (Sheffield: Almond Press, 1982; orig. 1926); David M. Gunn, *The Story of King David* (Sheffield: JSOT Press, 1978); James Van Seters, *Abraham in History and Tradition* (New Haven, Conn.: Yale University Press, 1978).

Chapter Five

From Story to Proclamation

Elijah, Amos, and Hosea

Read: 1 Kings 17–21; 2 Kings 1–2, 9–10;
Amos; Hosea

From the time of the divided monarchy we learn about an emerging phenomenon, that of explicit prophecy. While some of the leaders of the people had been called prophets (Abraham, Miriam, Aaron, Moses, et al.), it is not until the ninth century BCE that the Hebrew Scriptures mention prophetic activity. Considered the ancestor of prophecy in Jewish and Christian traditions, Elijah the Tishbite is introduced as a prophet of YHWH. The Scriptures describe him as a mysterious figure without parental name and without a grave; he dresses strangely, and in his lifestyle he is close to the Israel of old (1 Kings 17–19; 21). According to the biblical stories about him, he is an inflexible man, zealous for YHWH, who makes no compromise with Baalism. His name constitutes a confession of faith *'eli-jah,* "my God is YHWH." Thus, Queen Jezebel, who will not confess the god of Israel, never uses his name.[1] All the stories about him include coming and going; he is always on the move. Two mountain stories, one at Mt. Carmel (1 Kings 18:17–

46) and one at Mt. Horeb/Sinai (1 Kings 19:1–18) tell of
Elijah's prophetic activities.

In the first story Elijah shows the people in dramatic
fashion that YHWH, and not Baal, is god in Israel by
demonstrating YHWH's power over nature. In the second,
the prophet himself is shown that YHWH remains mysterious and unpredictable even to God's prophets in how
God reveals Godself. None of the theophanies of the past
(earthquake, fire, wind) let Elijah predict the one in the
present (a voice of gentle silence). There God commis-
sions him to anoint his successor, Elisha (1 Kings 19:15),
thus inaugurating a succession of prophets.

Prophecy and Prophetic Literature

According to Jeremiah 18:18, "instruction shall not per-
ish from the priest, nor counsel from the wise, nor the
word from the prophet." So the responsibility of a priest
is the teaching of Torah; the responsibility of a sage is to
provide counsel; and the responsibility of a prophet is the
word (*dabar*). The Hebrew word for prophet is *nabi'* from
the Akkadian *nabu'*, in the passive meaning "one who is
called" and in the active "one who is calling." Our English word "prophet" comes from the Greek *prophetes*. It
literally means "speaking for" or "before," which makes a
prophet a spokesperson for God and/or the people. Both
meanings inform the understandings of the character of
biblical prophets.

There have been numerous ways of classifying various
biblical prophets. They include:

+ *canonical: former and latter prophets*
  former: Joshua, Judges, Samuel, Kings
  latter: Isaiah, Jeremiah, Ezekiel, the Book of
      the Twelve

+ *historical: premonarchic and monarchic prophets*
  premonarchic: Abraham (Gen. 20), Aaron (Exod. 7),
      Miriam (Exod. 15), Deborah (Judg. 4–5), Moses
  monarchic:
      tenth century:
          Samuel, Nathan, Gad
      ninth century:
          Elijah, Elisha, Micaiah
      eighth century:
          Amos, Hosea, Isaiah of Jerusalem, Micah
      seventh century:
          Jeremiah, Zephaniah, Habakkuk, Nahum
      sixth century:
          Ezekiel, Second Isaiah/Deutero-Isaiah
      sixth–fifth centuries:
          Third Isaiah/Trito-Isaiah, Obadiah (?), Haggai,
          Zechariah
      fifth century:
          Joel, Malachi

+ *writing* and *nonwriting/preaching prophets*
  books attributed to prophets (Amos, Hosea, Isaiah, etc.)
  vs. stories about prophets (e.g., Elijah, Miriam, Nathan)

+ *central* vs. *peripheral prophets*[2]
  within the power structure of the establishment, to
  maintain the social order asking for changes within

the established order (e.g., Isaiah) vs. on the fringes of society to bring about social and religious change (e.g., Amos; Micah)

Prophecy is a well-known phenomenon in the Ancient Near East. Indeed, records about prophets and their activities exist in ancient Egypt, Canaan, Assyria, and Mesopotamia. As for the Israelites, prophecy emerges in the North. Indeed, the first southern prophet, Amos, will prophesy in the North.

The Book of Amos

The first prophet to whom a biblical book is attributed is the prophet Amos. The superscription — that is, the opening verse added later and functioning like a heading — of the book of Amos identifies him as among the shepherds of Tekoa, a small town fifteen miles south of Jerusalem (Amos 1:1). Not descending from a line of prophets, he is called to prophesy in the northern kingdom during the reign of Jeroboam II (Amos 7:10–17), probably around 760 BCE, a relatively peaceful time of great economic expansion for some; it was also a time of increasing poverty for most others. Whether Amos was a poor outcast or a wealthy well-educated person has divided interpreters through the ages. While some picture a humble shepherd clamoring for justice, others see him as a widely known tender of royal sheep who was well traveled and outspoken in taking a stance for ethical behavior. At the center of the controversy stands a verse from the biographical interlude and its possible interpretations.

Amos answered Amaziah, "I am no prophet, nor a prophet's son; but I am a herdsman, and a dresser of sycamore trees, and the LORD took me from following the flock, and the LORD said to me, 'Go, prophesy to my people Israel.'" (Amos 7:14)

Clearly a call narrative, the text does not give us any further direct descriptions of Amos's situation. Rather, we find several cycles of prophecies interrupted by several vision stories. For the prophecies, the language ascribed to Amos follows the general patterns of prophetic speech.[3] As messenger figures, prophets deliver oracles, often judgment speeches against those in power or the nation as a whole.

pattern of a judgment oracle:

1. introductory word: e.g., Hear this word..., As for you,..., Woe...

2. accusation/reason for the judgment that is to come: e.g., question, declarative, causal statement

   (a) naming the accusation

   (b) making it specific (elaboration)

3. messenger formula: "thus says YHWH" or simply "therefore"

4. announcement of judgment/punishment given by the deity (first- or third-person):

   (a) intervention

   (b) results of the intervention

Examples of all these types of prophecy abound throughout the prophetic literature. In the book of Amos oracles
against the nations (Amos 1:3–2:5) precede a series of
oracles against Israel (2:6–6:14) before giving way to five
visions (Amos 7:1–9:8b) surrounding a biographical interlude (Amos 7:10–17), and an epilogue (Amos 9:8c–15).
Traditional scholarship attributes most of the book to the
historical Amos, excluding the Judah editorial comments
(e.g., Amos 11:12: "Ephraim has surrounded me with lies,
and the house of Israel with deceit; but Judah still walks
with God, and is faithful to the Holy One"). The same can
be said for the doxologies (e.g., 4:13) and the epilogue.
Compared to the accusations leveled against the nations
surrounding Israel, the list of crimes of which the prophet
accuses Israel itself is much longer. It includes local and
social transgressions against Israelite community life, op-
pression of the poor internally, slavery, homelessness, etc.
(Amos 2:6–16). In a way, the remainder of the book can
be read as an elaboration of this one judgment oracle as
it delves into the specifics of social and ritual offenses
committed by the people who are accused of not living
up to expectations of just relationships among themselves
and with their god. Even though the term *berith*/covenant
itself is never uttered in the book, the theme of elec-
tion ("only you I have known . . . ") and a critical attitude
toward religious observances — "I hate, I despise your
festivals. . . . I will not accept your offerings" (5:21ff.); or
"come to Bethel — and transgress; to Gilgal — and multiply
your transgression" (4:4ff.), which is like saying "come to
church or synagogue — and sin" — contribute to uphold-
ing the tenets of the covenant at Sinai. Amos accuses the

people of neglecting God so badly that in the end he sees no hope for their redemption. The absence of hope remains noteworthy. Later readers of Amos found the original ending (Amos 9:8) too hard to bear, so that several generations of editors attempted to soften it (see Amos 9:8c–15). Most famously, Amos's proclamation is remembered for its focus on justice and righteousness.

I hate, I despise your festivals,
and I take no delight in your solemn assemblies.
Even though you offer me your burnt offerings and
    grain offerings,
I will not accept them;
and the offerings of well-being of your fatted animals
I will not look upon.
Take away from me the noise of your songs;
I will not listen to the melody of your harps.
But let justice roll down like waters,
and righteousness like an ever-flowing stream.
                                        (Amos 5:21–24)

The Hebrew word commonly translated as "justice" is *mishpat*. It appears four times in Amos, clustered in chapter 5 and once in chapter 6 (Amos 5:7, 15, 24; 6:12). In three of the four instances it occurs in parallelism with the Hebrew word *ṣedaqa* commonly translated as "righteousness." While the former is located in the judicial process — *mishpat* is done when the court successfully performs its duty (see Deut 25:1), the latter describes relational and contextual qualities of life of those who do right and live up to the norms of right relationships with God and with the

people. For Amos the two belong together; indeed, ṣedaqa
enables one to do justice.[4]

This gives us a taste of the prophecies of Amos. Like
Amos, the prophet Hosea prophesied in Israel, the northern
kingdom.

The Book of Hosea

Perhaps overlapping, or shortly after Amos, the prophet
Hosea prophesied during a period of decline of Israel, 750–
725 BCE, while Assyria was on the rise as a power in the
region.

After the death of Jeroboam II (745 BCE), his successor
Menahem voluntarily paid tribute to Tiglath-Pileser III of
Assyria to stay in power, which resulted in the people being
heavily taxed and the patriots in Israel resenting the king.
His successor Pekah starts out as anti-Assyrian; he supports
a coalition with Syria and the Philistines (Syro-Ephraimitic
coalition, 733), but when Judah refuses to join and ap-
peals to Assyria for help, Assyria under Tiglath-Pileser III
destroys the coalition with Syria, which was defeated in
732 BCE. Judah survives as a vassal state of Assyria for another ten years under a puppet king, Hoshea, who at first
acts as a faithful vassal to Assyria but then begins to look to
Egypt for help. When he withholds tribute, Shalmanezer V,
the new ruler of Assyria, attacks. Israel holds out for two
years; but Shalmanezer's successor Sargon II finally destroys Samaria, Israel's capital, in 722 BCE. The people
are deported, not as a group, but scattered throughout the
Assyrian empire. Thus the northern kingdom, Israel, comes
to an end. The prophet Hosea prophesies amid this turmoil,

bringing a message of judgment against the status quo and hope for a future beyond the present disastrous situation.

The book of Hosea is divided into three sections, each emphasizing a particular metaphor for the covenant between God and Israel. The first section of the book concentrates on the husband/wife metaphor. The marriage of Hosea to his promiscuous wife, Gomer, and the births of their three children parallel YHWH's tumultuous union with the faithless wife Israel. God's eventual reconciliation with "his wife" Israel hints at dynamics of domestic violence and provides a problematic model for Hosea's own reunion with Gomer (Hos. 1–3). The second and largest section takes up the parent/child metaphor for the God/Israel relationship. God alternates between the scolding, abusive, and the loving, caring parent, while Israel in its transgression of the covenant is the rebellious son (Hos. 4–11). The third and final section of the book, which is ascribed to the editorial work of Hosea's followers, interweaves both the husband/wife metaphor and the parent/rebellious son metaphor. The son is threatened with destruction, unless he repents. The repentant wife returns to her husband and to the land from whence she was banished (Hos. 12–14).

As for the final form of the book of Hosea, interpreters have struggled with the poor condition of the Hebrew text, which was very likely damaged during transmission. Also the relationship between chapters 1 and 3 and the remainder of the book has been debated, as has the relationship among the first three chapters.

Questions about the character of Gomer, Hosea's wife, and the nature of their marriage have abounded in traditional biblical scholarship. The most frequent ones include:

Was Gomer really a prostitute? If so, was she a temple prostitute, an ordinary whore, or merely an unfaithful wife? Did Hosea know he was marrying a promiscuous woman, or did Gomer's penchant for illicit affairs emerge only after their marriage? Showing more about the biases of the interpreters than the biblical text, these questions are matched by interpretations suggesting "solutions" to interpretive dilemmas of a biblical text that challenges traditional theologies. Some scholars interpret the marriage of Hosea and Gomer primarily as an allegory, thus preserving the possibility of Gomer's virtue by taking away her existence as an actual woman. Others think that Hosea literally married an unchaste woman, perhaps even a prostitute, and adopted the children conceived through her sexual encounters. Yet others interpret away the command to marry a promiscuous woman, claiming Gomer was chaste at the time of marriage but became unfaithful afterward, either as an adulterous wife, as an ordinary prostitute, or as a cultic prostitute. Some others try to vindicate Gomer's reputation by insisting that she should not be equated with the woman in Hosea 3, surmising that the prophet was bidden to take yet another wife who was unfaithful and whose infidelity is unfairly imposed upon Gomer.

By contrast, feminist and womanist interpretations have appealed to the ethical responsibility of interpreters (T. Drorah Setel), called for a diversity of biblical images (Renita J. Weems), and named the function of the biblical passage as the exposing of male sin (Phyllis Bird), on the one hand. On the other, they have shown the intricate rhetorical strategies that address the supposedly male audience as a "wanton woman," thus denying their manhood and putting them to shame (Yvonne Sherwood; Gale Yee). They all point out that the metaphor reinscribes realities for contemporary women and thus are dangerous to use without critique.[5]

Juxtaposed to these porno-prophetic passages, other passages in the book of Hosea highlight the vocabulary of love.

> The LORD said to me again, "Go, love a woman who has a lover and is an adulteress, just as the LORD loves the people of Israel, though they turn to other gods and love raisin cakes." (Hos. 3:1)

Discerning which love is the one that matters to God poses a challenge for Hosea as well as its readers. YHWH is portrayed as the one who alternately gives and withholds love, though the call to the people remains one-directional. A carefully crafted poem sums up this theology of "love":

> When Israel was a child, I loved him,
> and out of Egypt I called my son.
> The more I called them,
> the more they went from me;
> they kept sacrificing to the Baals,
> and offering incense to idols.
> Yet it was I who taught Ephraim to walk,
> I took them up in my arms;
> but they did not know that I healed them.
> I led them with cords of human kindness,
> with bands of love.
> I was to them like those who
> lift infants to their cheeks.
> I bent down to them and fed them.

They shall return to the land of Egypt,
and Assyria shall be their king,
because they have refused to return to me.
The sword rages in their cities,
it consumes their oracle-priests,
and devours because of their schemes.
My people are bent on turning away from me.
To the Most High they call,
but he does not raise them up at all.
How can I give you up, Ephraim?
How can I hand you over, O Israel?
How can I make you like Admah?
How can I treat you like Zeboiim?
My heart recoils within me;
my compassion grows warm and tender.
I will not execute my fierce anger;
I will not again destroy Ephraim;
for I am God and no mortal/not a man,
the Holy One in your midst,
and I will not come in wrath. (Hos. 11:1–9)

God as mother of Israel/Ephraim shows compassion instead of anger, claiming that divine holiness conquers divine wrath. Thus the poem is part of the promise that counters the judgment oracles with their cruel claims and pornographic imagery (e.g., Hos. 2:2–7; 9:1–6). Unlike Amos, Hosea insists that beyond destruction there is the promise of historical salvation; there is hope and healing after the suffering because God insists on "being known" and present in the midst of the people (Hos. 11:9).

Study Questions

1. In terms of forms, classifications, etc., what constitutes biblical prophecy?
2. How did biblical prophecy emerge?
3. What have you learned about the prophet Elijah?
4. What characterizes the book of Amos?
5. Who was Amos the prophet?
6. What characterizes the book of Hosea?
7. Who was Hosea the prophet?

Further Reading

Brueggemann, Walter. *Prophetic Imagination*. Revised and updated ed. Minneapolis: Augsburg Fortress, 2001.

Dempsey, Carol J. *The Prophets: A Liberation-Critical Reading*. Minneapolis: Fortress Press, 2000.

Notes

1. Phyllis Trible, "Exegesis for Storytellers and Other Strangers," *Journal of Biblical Literature* 114, no. 1 (1995): 3–19.

2. Robert Wilson, *Prophecy and Society in Ancient Israel* (Philadelphia: Fortress Press, 1980).

3. Claus Westermann, *Basic Forms of Prophetic Speech* (Philadelphia: Westminster Press, 1967; orig. 1961).

4. Klaus Koch, *The Prophets I: The Assyrian Period* (Philadelphia: Fortress Press, 1983; orig. 1972).

5. T. Drorah Setel, "Prophets and Pornography," in
Feminist Interpretation of the Bible, ed. Letty Russell (Phila-
delphia: Westminster Press, 1985), 86–95; Renita J.
Weems, "Gomer: Victim of Violence or Victim of Meta-
phor?" *Semeia* 47 (1989): 87–104; see also her *Battered
Love: Marriage, Sex, and Violence in the Hebrew Prophets*,
Overtures to Biblical Theology (Minneapolis: Fortress
Press, 1995); Phyllis Bird, "To Play the Harlot: An In-
quiry into an Old Testament Metaphor," in *Gender and
Difference in Ancient Israel*, ed. Peggy Day (Minneapolis:
Fortress Press, 1989), 75–94; Yvonne Sherwood, *The Pros-
titute and the Prophet: Hosea's Marriage in Literary-Theoretical
Perspective*, Gender, Culture, Theory 2 (Sheffield: Shef-
field Academic Press, 1996); Gale Yee, "The Book of
Hosea: Introduction, Commentary, and Reflections," *New
Interpreter's Bible* 7 (Nashville: Abingdon Press, 1996),
195–297.

Chapter Six

Prophetic Words and Actions

Isaiah of Jerusalem, Micah, and Jeremiah

Read: Isaiah 1–12; 36–39; Micah; Jeremiah 1–6; 9–20; 30–31; 44

In the eighth century BCE, biblical prophets come in pairs. We have witnessed the proclamations of the prophets Amos and Hosea in the northern kingdom, Israel. Now with Isaiah of Jerusalem and Micah of Moresheth we find ourselves in the southern kingdom, Judah, during the second half of the eighth century BCE. Here the reign of King Uzziah (783–742 BCE) was just as successful as that of Jeroboam II in the North, resulting in a most prosperous period in Judah's history.

Uzziah reorganized Judah's army and led it on several successful campaigns. Uzziah's successor Jotham (742–735 BCE) continued Uzziah's policies and enjoyed similar success. Jotham was followed by Ahaz (735–715 BCE), who responded to the Assyrian threat to the region by refusing to join the anti-Assyrian alliance and became an Assyrian vassal instead, which "assured" the survival of the southern kingdom as a nation under the Assyrian empire. Ahaz was succeeded by Hezekiah (715–687 BCE), who began plotting with the Philistines, Egyptians, and Babylonians against Assyria. Isaiah of Jerusalem had a lot to say to Hezekiah. Hezekiah's intent to revolt led to the Assyrians' marching against Judah under Sennacherib, capturing forty-six cities in Judah before they began their siege of Jerusalem, which they broke off in 701 BCE. Though Jerusalem did not fall to Assyria, Judah had to pay an increased tribute, and Hezekiah had to swear allegiance to Assyria. So it is the kings Jotham, Ahaz, and Hezekiah that the prophet Isaiah of Jerusalem contends with — as does the prophet Micah, who prophesied during the last quarter of the eighth century in Judah as well (725–701 BCE).

Isaiah of Jerusalem is one of the prophets we meet in the book of Isaiah (Isa. 1–39). The others are Isaiah of the Exile, also known as Second or Deutero-Isaiah (Isa. 40–55), and possibly Isaiah of the Return, also known as Third or Trito-Isaiah (Isa. 56–66). Their worlds, their hopes and fears, their theologies, their prophecies, are all gathered under the name of *Isaiah, yes(h)a' yahu,* "God/YHWH is salvation."[1]

Historical, literary, and theological observations suggest these major divisions. While the historical references to Judean kings and Assyrian politics locate Isaiah 1–39 in the eighth century BCE, it is references to Nebuchadrezzar, the exile in Babylon, and King Cyrus of Persia that place Isaiah 40–66 in the sixth century BCE. In terms of literary genres, chapters 1–39 contain primarily oracles of judgment, while in chapters 40–66 oracles of salvation predominate. Theologically, the entire book emphasizes the holiness of God; in Isaiah 1–39 the people's apostasy leads to an inevitable *yom YHWH,* a day of judgment; meanwhile God's holiness permeates God's actions as creator and redeemer in Isaiah 40–66.

The chapters of the book ascribed to Isaiah of Jerusalem comprise a collection of primarily judgment oracles against Judah and Israel, interspersed with a call narrative (Isa. 6), oracles against the foreign nations (Isa. 13–19), some postexilic apocalyptic materials (Isa. 24–27), and conclude with a historical account of Hezekiah's deliverance from the Assyrians that parallels 2 Kings 18–20.

Isaiah, whose name contains a confession of faith just as does Elijah's (see page 73 above), is a citizen of Jerusalem with access to the royal court and the temple. His call comes at a precise moment in the history of Judah, "in the year King Uzziah died," 742 BCE (Isa. 6:1). Uzziah died from leprosy — a theological challenge to the Deuteronomistic historians since he was a good and faithful king (2 Kings 14:21–15:34), credited with developing agriculture, modernizing the army, increasing trade, and promoting devout YHWH worship (2 Chron. 26). Isaiah of Jerusalem probably admired King Uzziah, as the clear relationship between Uzziah's death and the call of the prophet shows (Isa. 6:1–4). In the year when King Uzziah died, Isaiah saw *the* king, YHWH, the Holy One, on a throne:

In the year that King Uzziah died, I saw the LORD sitting on a throne, high and lofty; and the hem of his robe filled the temple. Seraphs were in attendance above him; each had six wings: with two they covered their faces, and with two they covered their feet, and with two they flew, and one called to another and

said: "Holy, holy, holy is the LORD of hosts/*YHWH
Ṣebaoth*; the whole earth is full of his glory."
    The pivots on the thresholds shook at the voices
of those who called, and the house filled with smoke.

Language of vision and seeing in the smoke-filled temple
recalls Exodus imagery both in the veiling and unveil-
ing. YHWH's holiness fills not only the temple but the
entire earth.
    A cleansing ritual ensues (Isa. 6:6–7) and readies the
prophet for his call and commissioning (Isa. 6:8–10).

Then one of the seraphs flew to me, holding a live
coal that had been taken from the altar with a pair of
tongs. The seraph touched my mouth with it and said:
"Now that this has touched your lips, your guilt has
departed and your sin is blotted out." Then I heard
the voice of the LORD saying, "Whom shall I send,
and who will go for us?" And I said, "Here am I; send
me!" (Isa. 6:6–8)

The visionary gives way to the auditory, and Isaiah hears
YHWH's dangerous question, "Whom shall I send, and
who will go for us?" to which he answers almost too fast,
"Here am I; send me!" To this, YHWH replies: "Go and
say to this people:

'Keep listening, but do not comprehend;
keep looking, but do not understand.'
Make the mind of this people dull,
and stop their ears,
and shut their eyes,
so that they may not look with their eyes,

> and listen with their ears,
> and comprehend with their minds,
> and turn and be healed."
> Then I said, "How long, O Lord?"
>   (Isa. 6:9–11a)

As the prophet realizes the extent of his commission ("my people" have become "this people" (Isa. 6:9–10), he is less than sure that he really wants to accept the divine call: "How long, O LORD?" (Isa. 6:11–13). Nevertheless, the book assumes that he does.

Isaiah's career is one of the longest prophetic careers, spanning the years 742–701 BCE (including times of withdrawal from prophesying when the king in power did not pay heed). In chapters 1–5, Isaiah calls the people to reason (see Isa. 1:18–20); Israel is described as a "rebellious son" — if we are paying attention to gendered language, this is important to note. (If we were to read this text in the liturgy, we would probably make it inclusive and say "children" or "offspring"; but then we are left with images of both male and female young ones, and only female images when we move to accusations of promiscuity in Isa. 1:21). Lamenting the injustice, the prophet juxtaposes the present to an eschatological vision/future expectation "in the days to come." The "swords into plowshares" passage (Isa. 2:2–4), made famous by peace movements around the globe, finds its parallel in Micah 4:1–3; it clearly expresses the hope of a people in the midst of imperial hostilities.

> In days to come the mountain of the LORD's house
>   shall be established
> as the highest of the mountains,

and shall be raised above the hills;
all the nations shall stream to it.
Many peoples shall come and say,
"Come, let us go up to the mountain of the LORD,
to the house of the God of Jacob;
that he may teach us his ways and
that we may walk in his paths."
For out of Zion shall go forth instruction/*torah*
And the word of the LORD from Jerusalem.
He shall judge between the nations,
and shall arbitrate for many peoples;
they shall beat their swords into plowshares,
and their spears into pruning hooks;
nation shall not lift up sword against nation,
neither shall they learn war any more. (Isa. 2:2–4)

Right after this passage, the oracles revert to judgment speeches denouncing social injustice. Threat of destruction and political crisis and the human need and ability to perceive and speak out give rise to a promise (Isa. 7:1–17), familiar to Christians from the Advent readings.

Again the LORD spoke to Ahaz, saying, "Ask a sign of the LORD your God; let it be deep as Sheol or high as heaven." But Ahaz said, "I will not ask, and I will not put the LORD to the test." Then Isaiah said: "Hear then, O house of David! Is it too little for you to weary mortals, that you weary my God also? Therefore the LORD himself will give you a sign. Look, the young woman is with child and shall bear a son, and shall name him Immanuel ['God with us']. He shall eat curds and honey by the time he knows how to refuse the evil and choose the good. For before the child knows how to refuse the evil and choose the good, the land before whose two kings you are in dread will be deserted. The LORD will bring on you and on your people and on your ancestral house such days as have not come since the day that Ephraim departed from Judah — the king of Assyria." (Isa. 7:10–17)

What is the promised sign? A pregnant young woman? A male child? The name of the child, Immanuel/God with us? The food of the child? All of the above?

In Christian tradition the promised sign has led to retrospective readings, though Isaiah is talking in and about his time and not about Mary and Jesus of Nazareth. The word *betulah,* a "young woman of marriageable age," was translated by the Septuagint as *parthenos* and consequently by the Vulgate as *virgo.* Such incorrect translation has had lamentable consequences in doctrinal struggles regarding a virgin birth. To the contrary, Isaiah of Jerusalem is very clearly addressing a political situation in the eighth century BCE. He advises the king to part from Assyria.

When the king doesn't heed Isaiah's advice, the prophet withdraws. The book of Isaiah does not record any activity of the prophet until the coronation in 715 BCE of King Hezekiah, who is known as a king walking "in the footsteps of David." He promotes the suppression of places of Canaanite worship as well as the purification of Jerusalem worship; he is also credited with the construction of a tunnel at Siloam, on the outskirts of Jerusalem, that will give the city access to water when under siege.

When in 705 BCE King Sargon of Assyria dies, a chain reaction of revolution throughout the Assyrian empire is set in motion. Against Isaiah's advice King Hezekiah joins in with the revolt (10:5–19); judgment follows as we learn that a hostile nation is used as God's instrument (see 30:15–17): "Assyria, the rod of my anger." In 701 BCE, Sargon's successor Sennacherib invades Jerusalem (see 31:4–5, 8–9). Isaiah is proposing YHWH will protect Jerusalem, counting on the continuity of the Davidic line (see 2 Sam. 7). Surprisingly, Assyria withdraws, and Judah is left weakened but still independent (see 2 Kings 19) when Isaiah leaves the scene in 701 BCE.

Overall, the proclamation of Isaiah of Jerusalem does not offer political solutions to the spiritual challenges of how to allow God's holiness to fill every aspect of life. Speaking about much judgment and some promise of salvation, and portraying God as punishing as well as caring, abusive as well as compassionate, Isaiah of Jerusalem introduces the concept of a faithful remnant, a concept that will become even more important in the latter parts of the book of Isaiah.

The Book of Micah

Meanwhile, the other prophet in eighth-century Judah who left us a book is Micah of Moresheth. His name means "who is like YHWH?" and suggests a rhetorical question. From the hill country of Judah twenty-five miles northwest of Jerusalem, Micah expresses his dislike of cities in general and of Jerusalem in particular. Indeed, he hated Jerusalem.

He prophesied in the last quarter of the eighth century, 725–701 BCE, overlapping with Isaiah of Jerusalem.[2]

Patterns of juxtaposed judgment and salvation oracles, similar to those of Isaiah of Jerusalem, shape the book of Micah, which in the first part is addressed to a universal audience (Mic. 1–5): "Hear, you peoples, all of you; listen, O earth, all that is in it" (Mic. 1:2). He then turns to Israel/Judah (Mic. 6–7).

The first biblical prophet to denounce the demise of Jerusalem (Mic. 3:9–12) — a fact that later will save Jeremiah's life on one occasion (Jer. 38) — Micah sets himself over against all prophets who do not live for justice:

> Thus says the LORD concerning the prophets
> who lead my people astray,
> who cry "Peace"
> when they have something to eat,
> but declare war against those
> who put nothing into their mouths. . . .
> But as for me, I am filled with power,
> with the spirit of the LORD,
> and with justice and might,
> to declare to Jacob his transgression
> and to Israel his sin. (Mic. 3:5–8)

Claiming charismatic powers ("I am filled with the spirit of the LORD"), he chastises the leadership for fostering injustice while pretending faithfulness through their worship practices. Again and again, Micah calls the leaders and the people in general to return to the commitments and commandments of the Sinai covenant.

The best-known passage of the book of Micah summa-
rizes the prophet's proclamation:

Hear what the LORD says:
Rise, plead your case before the mountains,
and let the hills hear your voice.
Hear, you mountains, the controversy of the LORD,
and you enduring foundations of the earth;
for the LORD has a controversy with his people,
and he will contend with Israel.
"O my people, what have I done to you?
In what have I wearied you? Answer me!
For I brought you up from the land of Egypt,
and redeemed you from the house of slavery;
and I sent before you Moses, Aaron, and Miriam.
O my people, remember now what King Balak of
        Moab devised,
What Balaam son of Beor answered him,
and what happened from Shittim to Gilgal,
That you may know the saving acts of the LORD."
"With what shall I come before the LORD,
and bow myself before God on high?
Shall I come before him with burnt offerings,
with calves a year old?
Will the LORD be pleased with thousands of rams,
with ten thousands of rivers of oil?
Shall I give my firstborn for my transgression,
the fruit of my body for the sin of my soul?"
He told you, O mortal, what is good;
and what does the LORD require of you
but to do justice, and to love kindness,

and to walk humbly with your God? (Mic. 6:1–8)

Invoking the ancestors of the Exodus, including Miriam (Mic. 6:4), he asks Israel to live by the Sinai covenant, emphasizing what is "good": to do *mishpat* (justice), to love *hesed* (covenant loyalty/kindness), and to walk humbly with God (Mic. 6:8). Micah's prophetic activity breaks off with the siege of Jerusalem. What follows in the biblical record after the sudden withdrawal in 701 BCE by Sennacherib is *prophetic silence*, which will last for almost three quarters of the seventh century.

Toward Jeremiah

The break in reported prophetic messages is not matched by political or economic inactivity. Upon the death of King Hezekiah in 687 BCE, King Manasseh came to the throne. He paid homage to Assyria, erected altars to Assyrian deities, and is said to have supported sacred prostitution and allowed child sacrifices, none of which is documented elsewhere. Contradicting all Deuteronomistic theology, he ruled for fifty-five years and died peacefully. His successor Amon, on the other hand, was assassinated after two years.

Then in 640 BCE King Josiah comes to the throne at the age of eight years. When he has grown older, he initiates a reformation back to a purer Yahwism. In 621 BCE he orders the repair of the temple structure. There a scroll turns up, the so-called Temple Scroll, which rather conveniently legitimates Josiah's actions (2 Kings 22:3–13). Some have speculated that this document was hidden in the temple for safe keeping during the anti-Deuternonomic climate of King Manasseh's reign. The scroll is authenticated by Huldah the prophet (2 Kings 22:14–20). She judges it to be a scroll of authority, and her authentication becomes the basis for a reformation in the land. It leads to the purging of the non-Yahwistic cults and practices, the suppression of divination and magic, the destruction of the shrines of the North, Israel, and to the closing of outlying shrines in Judah to centralize all public worship in Jerusalem again.

As for the content of the Temple Scroll, Jerome is credited with suggesting in the fourth century CE that its text was probably the book of Deuteronomy, chapters 12–26. Others have suspected that it included additional chapters, comprising the larger section Deuteronomy 5–28.

The Book of Deuteronomy

Presented as a farewell speech by Moses to the people of Israel, delivered before his death, the book of Deuteronomy takes its name in the Septuagint from Deuteronomy 17:18, *deuteros nomos*, meaning "a copy of the law."[3] It opens with a recital of the mighty acts of God on behalf of Israel as they journeyed from Mount Horeb to Jordan. Then, based on this shared history, an admonition follows: Moses calls the people to obey the "statutes and ordinances" (Deut. 1–4). A restatement of Torah makes up the core of the book (Deut. 5–28). It contains regulations concerning many parts of life, including the Ten Commandments (Deut. 5:6–21) and the *shema* (Deut. 6:4–9), one of the oldest creeds in the Bible. The Deuteronomic Code itself (Deut. 12–26) states the regulations upon Israel's communal life with interspersed homiletic comments. The section concludes with a series of blessings and curses (Deut. 27–28). A hortatory sermon, calling the people to decision (Deut. 29–30), and several chapters on the passing of leadership (Deut. 31), the song of Moses (Deut. 32), the blessing of Moses (Deut. 33), and the death of Moses (Deut. 34) conclude the book.

Deuteronomy is an exercise in inner-biblical interpretation. It takes the ancient traditions of the Mosaic age (see the book of Exodus) and restates them in a way that makes them vital for later generations, addressing the children of the ancestors to bridge the gap to those who question the relevance of Sinai for the current generation. The book explores the tension between the then, the now, and the not-yet. Its theology provides models for meaning-making in the seventh century (and beyond), a time during which prophetic voices are scarce (Zephaniah, Nahum, Habakkuk) until the last decade or so of the seventh century BCE, when we hear the voice of the prophet Jeremiah.

The Book of Jeremiah

The book of Jeremiah comes to us as a collection of laments, proclamations of judgment, and a few powerful eschatological promises, interspersed with stories about the life of the prophet toward the end of the seventh century BCE until the destruction of Jerusalem in 587 BCE. Born or called in 626 BCE, Jeremiah comes from a priestly family in Anathoth in the territory of Benjamin, outside Jerusalem; by his family lineage he has an anti-monarchical position.

If 626 is the date of his call, one wonders why the prophet does not have anything to say about Josiah's reformation. Even the Deuteronomistic editorial layer does not add any comments there. Biblical scholars have debated the composition of the book and the identity/ies of the prophet Jeremiah for a long time. The leading theories on how the book was put together either assume three sources or authors, or posit two scrolls that were eventually combined, or propose various editors at various times.[4] Alternative interpretations have mostly dealt with the book in its final form. Feminist and womanist interpreters focus on the numerous layers of female imagery, on the gendering of power dynamics, and on descriptions of sexual violence.[5] Postcolonial readers emphasize instances of resistance to the empires of the time, Assyria, Babylon, and Persia. LGBTQ perspectives highlight the fluidity of gender dynamics in Jeremiah and the sexual connotations in interchanges between God and prophet.[6]

The historical events during Jeremiah's career take a rapid turn for the worse after Assyria falls to the Babylonians in 612 BCE. Squashed in the tectonic movements of the empires, Josiah dies in battle at Megiddo in 609 BCE when he tries to stop the Egyptians under Pharaoh Necho II from reaching Nineveh. For the next five years Judah becomes a vassal power to Egypt until the Egyptians are beaten by the Babylonians at the battle of Carchemish in 605 BCE. It takes until 598 BCE, when the Babylonians take over Judah. In a first deportation the Babylonians take the upper classes, including royal and temple personnel, into exile in Babylon. Vassal king Zedekiah becomes the last king of Judah; after a siege, Jerusalem is destroyed in 587 BCE. A second deportation ensues. It is into this turmoil, this redrawing of international boundaries, that the prophecies of Jeremiah are spoken. The book of Jeremiah is a collection of poetry and prose, with much of the prose ascribed to sixth-century Deuteronomistic editors. The poetic oracles in the book appear in no clear chronological sequence. Scholars have also noted considerable variation in length and order between the Hebrew of the Massoretic text and the Greek of the Septuagint.[7] Further, there has been debate as to how many sayings to ascribe to the historical Jeremiah.[8]

The book of Jeremiah opens with the call of the prophet (Jer. 1:4–19). It offers insights into the intimate as well as destructive nature of his prophecy.

> Now the word of the LORD came to me saying,
> "Before I formed you in the womb I knew you,
> and before you were born I consecrated you/set you
> apart;
> I appointed you a prophet to the nations." (Jer. 1:5)

Initiated by divine first-person speech, the call proclaims the mystery of Jeremiah's birth and destiny. In retrospect Jeremiah sees his life determined by YHWH, "known" and "set apart" — both special and isolated; in a sense Jeremiah's whole life is a life of isolation in obedience to YHWH. He is isolated from his family, from any social life, even from the religious system of his land. Commissioned from the divine womb to be an international messenger prophesying the word of God, Jeremiah is the first prophet called beyond the land of Israel/Judah ("a prophet to the nations"). As is typical for call narratives, he resists: "Truly I do not know how to speak, for I am only a boy" (Jer. 1:6) — only to receive assurances (Jer. 1:7–9) and the commission,

> "See, today I appoint you over nations and over
>   kingdoms,
> to pluck up and to pull down,
> to destroy and to overthrow,
> to build and to plant." (Jer. 1:10)

Four words of destruction and two words of rebuilding fit well Jeremiah's prophecy, which is weighted on the side of destruction.

Following the call of Jeremiah, two concerns predominate: religious corruption of the time and Judah's insensitivity to the covenant (e.g., Jer. 2:1–13). Like Hosea, Jeremiah employs the metaphor of marriage, accusing the people of acting as YHWH's unfaithful wife. Jeremiah keeps struggling with his identification with the people, and his role as a prophet over against the people (see especially the so-called confessions of Jeremiah: 11:18–23; 12:1–6; 15:10–11, 15–20; 17:14–18; 18:18–23; 20:7–13).

Eschatological passages counter the onslaught of judgment oracles, especially in chapters 30–31, which Luther called "the Little Book of Hope." There fundamental reversals are promised: women mourners (Jer. 9:17–23) will turn into dancers (Jer. 31:2–6), a new creation will entail a turnaround of oppressive gender dynamics (Jer. 31:20–22), and a new covenant will right the people's relationship with YHWH forever (Jer. 31:31–34).

Hope, however, is quickly squashed as the book returns to more judgment. We learn that Jeremiah's prophecies of doom are not well received: the mob is about to kill him when he leaves Jerusalem; he is, however, captured and imprisoned (Jer. 37:11–38:6). When the Babylonians capture Jerusalem, Jeremiah is ordered out of prison by Nebuchadrezzar. As the second deportation takes place, a small group chooses to flee to Egypt and forces Jeremiah to come along (Jer. 43:1–7); there he disappears. The book of Jeremiah goes on with the oracles against the nations (Jer. 46–51) and concludes with a historical appendix on the destruction of Jerusalem and the deportation to Babylon (Jer. 52; see also 2 Kings 24:18–25:30).

As a point of caution, the rhetoric used to express Jeremiah's message of having strayed from God's way is full of powerful and problematic images. Addressed to a predominantly male audience, gendered and racialized metaphors invite the hearers to imagine being raped by divine power and shamed publicly (Jer. 13:20–27). While one can only speculate about the effectiveness in ancient times of rhetorical strategies that publicly shame their audiences into exhibiting changed behavior by means of misogynous, effeminizing, and racist accusations, modern psychology has taught us that shaming evokes feelings of inadequacy and inferiority, rejection and powerlessness, quite opposite from the strength needed for the challenging work of change. Indeed, we need to hold the challenges of judgment together with the hopeful promises to do this complex book justice and mine it for our contemporary contexts.

Study Questions

1. What have you learned about the book of Isaiah?
2. Who was Isaiah of Jerusalem?
3. How would you characterize the theology of Isaiah 1–39?
4. What characterizes the book of Micah?
5. Who was Micah of Moresheth?
6. How do you understand the book of Jeremiah?
7. Who was Jeremiah the prophet?

Further Reading

Holladay, William L. *Unbound by Time: Isaiah Still Speaks.* Cambridge: Cowley, 2002.

Commentaries on Isaiah, Micah, and Jeremiah, in the commentaries recommended above on page 25.

Notes

1. See Brevard S. Childs, *Isaiah,* Old Testament Library (Louisville: Westminster John Knox Press, 2001), for more detail.

2. Cf. Delbert R. Hillers, *Micah: A Commentary on the Book of the Prophet Micah,* Hermeneia (Philadelphia: Fortress Press, 1984).

3. See Patrick D. Miller, *Deuteronomy,* Interpretation: A Bible Commentary for Teaching and Preaching (Louisville: John Knox Press, 1990), for further exposition of these homilies.

4. Bernhard Duhm, *Das Buch Jeremia*, Kurzer Hand-Commentar zum Alten Testament 11 (Leipzig: J. C. B. Mohr, 1901); Sigmund Mowinckel, *Zur Komposition des Buches Jeremia* (Kristiana: Dybwad, 1914); William L. Holladay, *Jeremiah 1* and *Jeremiah 2*, Hermeneia (Philadelphia and Minneapolis: Fortress Press, 1986 and 1989); Robert P. Carroll, *Jeremiah: A Commentary*, Old Testament Library (Philadelphia: Westminster Press, 1986).

5. Kathleen M. O'Connor, "Jeremiah," in *The Women's Bible Commentary*, ed. Carol A. Newsom and Sharon H. Ringe (Louisville: Westminster John Knox Press, 1992), 169–77; Renita J. Weems, *Battered Love: Marriage, Sex, and Violence in the Hebrew Prophets*, Overtures to Biblical Theology (Minneapolis: Fortress Press, 1995); Angela Bauer, *Gender in the Book of Jeremiah: A Feminist-Literary Reading*, Studies in Biblical Literature 5 (New York: Peter Lang, 1999).

6. Angela Bauer-Levesque, "Jeremiah," in *The Queer Bible Commentary*, ed. Deryn Guest et al. (London: SCM Press, 2006), 386–93.

7. The Septuagint contains more actual words, while omitting one-eighth of the Massoretic text. Further, the oracles against the nations are placed differently within the book.

8. John Bright assumes the most *ipsissima verba*, Robert Carroll the least, with the other commentators falling somewhere in between. See John Bright, *Jeremiah*, Anchor Bible 21 (Garden City, N.Y.: Doubleday, 1965); Carroll, *Jeremiah: A Commentary*.

Chapter Seven

Prophetic Visions from Exile

Ezekiel and Deutero-Isaiah

Read: Ezekiel 1–3; 7–9; 18; 20; 34; 37; Isaiah 40–66

We have moved with the people of Judah through the seventh century BCE and traveled with Jeremiah into "the Exile." What does exile involve? What does this experience mean for the people of Israel? Exile is not just a historical experience, but a concept, a way of seeing the world. It means feeling like a stranger, feeling alienated, carrying a sense of betrayal. Read from the perspective of exile, the Bible is a response to a sense of massive betrayal in the face of history. Why has our God allowed this to happen? Why do we suffer? Where is our salvation? Indeed, read from a perspective of exile — and there is research to underscore that most of the Hebrew Bible was put together in its current edited form during exile and shortly thereafter[1] — the Bible is better understood as a magnificent response to disaster.

The children of Israel's faith did not disappear in a situation of crisis, but deepened. The Bible shows a people bound inextricably to one land; yet the Bible throughout history has been read outside that land. Despite the promise of the land, Judaism began as a diaspora religion. Judaism

began in exile. Jews are the descendants of the inhabitants
of Yehud (the Persian name for what was formerly known
as Judah) after the destruction of the nation.

In the Bible the Exile is presented as punishment, disaster, separation from God. Yet it is the "historical norm."
We are looking here at something that never should have
happened in terms of the theology of Israel, something literally unthinkable. There had been this covenant with David
that was to last forever and ever (2 Sam. 7; Ps. 48:13–15).
But now the temple is destroyed, the priesthood has been
exiled, the people live in a foreign land (Ps. 44:9–16).

In 597 BCE, Nebuchadrezzar marches against Judah and
succeeds. The first deportation takes the king, the members of the court, the civil and military leaders as well as
the temple establishment — including Ezekiel — to exile in
Babylon. Zedekiah is made king.

An uprising in Babylon in 595/594 BCE made life for
Jews more difficult as the Exile progressed. Open conspiracy
in the west including Judah, Tyre, and Amon with Egyptian
backing in 598/588 BCE, elicits Nebuchadrezzar's reaction.
He strikes back besieging Jerusalem in January 588 BCE;
after eighteen months of siege Jerusalem falls in August
587 BCE. The temple is destroyed, and a second major deportation to Babylon follows (2 Kings 24:18–25:30, with
the parallel report in Jer. 52). While the two biblical ac-
counts cannot be harmonized satisfactorily in terms of
numbers, we assume that this second deportation left the
society of Judah/Yehud in complete disarray, as major con-
flicts upon the return after 538 BCE make evident (Isa.
56–66).

In exile, the Jewish people settled down after a while, chiefly in the city of Babylon, where they were used as laborers in Nebuchadrezzar's building programs. They were allowed to stay together as communities. There is no indication that they were subjected to harsh treatment. They were allowed to worship and to live in peace as long as they respected the Babylonian law. They corresponded with the remnant back in Jerusalem, back in "the land" (Jer. 29). The language they spoke was Aramaic at the time. Indeed, there was a certain freedom for exiled Judah/Yehud as long as they were obedient to Babylon; they were even allowed to engage in agricultural pursuits, business, and commercial endeavors.[2]

Thus, unlike their ancestors in Egypt, the Babylonian exiles did not experience extreme external suffering. Nevertheless, they found themselves in a crisis, a crisis of meaning, a spiritual crisis:

By the rivers of Babylon —
there we sat down and there we wept
when we remembered Zion.
On the willows there we hung up our harps.
For there our captors asked us for songs,
and our tormentors asked for mirth, saying,
"Sing us one of the songs of Zion!"
How could we sing the LORD's song in a foreign land?

(Ps. 137:1–4)

What does it mean for YHWH that the temple has been destroyed? What does is mean for the chosen people? Is YHWH not all-powerful? Is YHWH dead, or asleep? Are the Babylonian deities stronger after all? Does the fault lie with us, with our sins, or with the sins of our parents? And what about the prophecies of the past two hundred years? What about the promise of a messiah (see Isaiah of Jerusalem)? How long will this go on? And after this, who is the true Israel? As you can imagine, there were differing responses to the experiences of exile. In the remainder of this chapter and in the next we shall explore some of them.

The Book of Ezekiel

Among the prophets, not only Jeremiah, but also the prophet Ezekiel crosses the bridge between preexilic Israel and exilic times. The son of a priest and a priest himself, the prophet Ezekiel was part of the first deportation in 597 BCE. He received his call in Babylon in 593 BCE (Ezek. 1:4–3:14) in a complex vision and an auditory commission. The imagery and language are also found in the call of Moses (Exod. 3) and the call of Isaiah of Jerusalem (Isa. 6) as well as elsewhere in the Bible (Ps. 18:8–14; Judg. 14:18; Deut. 28:49; Jer. 48:40; Prov. 14:4). In their combination, however, they are unique to Ezekiel. Through the ages they have been considered anything from bizarre to obscure and unintelligible, so much so that the rabbis forbade anyone under the age of thirty to read the first chapter of the book of Ezekiel. Following his vision and commission, Ezekiel swallows a scroll (Ezek. 2:10–3:4). After eating the scroll the prophet has no further responsibility than to proclaim; stuffed with the message he has to prophesy regardless.

He spread it before me; it had writing on the front
and on the back, and on it were words of lamentation
and mourning and woe. He said to me, "O mortal, eat
what is offered to you; eat this scroll, and go, speak to
the house of Israel." So I opened my mouth, and he
gave me the scroll to eat. He said to me, "Mortal, eat
this scroll that I give you and fill your stomach with
it." Then I ate it; and in my mouth it was as sweet
as honey. He said to me: "Mortal, go to the house of
Israel and speak my very words to them."

God's message through Ezekiel is one of the transcendence
and holiness of YHWH whom the people are supposed to
"know" ("so that they know that I am YHWH"). We learn
that Ezekiel was visited by the elders in the community
to receive the word. He lived in his own house and was
married. His wife is said to have died on the eve of the
destruction of Jerusalem in 587 BCE. Told by YHWH not
to weep (Ezek. 24:15–24), the prophet sees her death as a
symbol.

Ezekiel's oracles are extremely long, quite detailed, and
often repetitious (3:17–19//33:1–9; ch. 16//23, containing
some of the most misogynous and pornographic passages
in the Bible). They proclaim doom against Jerusalem and
Judah (Ezek. 3:16–24:27) and judgments against the foreign nations (Ezek. 25–32). Their literary style suggests
that they were probably written first rather than spoken.[3]
Allegories, symbolic acts and visions are prominent; char-
acteristic forms of prophetic speech used by the earlier
prophets do not appear often. Then after the fall of Jerusalem and the destruction of the temple in 587 BCE,

Ezekiel's proclamation shifts to talk about promises of a future restoration of a nation (Ezek. 37) and the temple (Ezek. 40–44).

> Thus says the Lord GOD: I am going to open your graves, O my people; and I will bring you back to the land of Israel. And you shall know that I am the LORD, when I open your graves, and bring you up from your graves, O my people. I will put my spirit within you, and you shall live, and I will place you on your own soil; then you shall know that I, the LORD, have spoken and will act, says the LORD. (Ezek. 37:12–14)

To a people in utter despair, the prophet offers a vision of a transcendent God, the Holy One, whom no words are able to describe adequately. This divine power is mediated through the spirit of YHWH; and the purpose of God's revelation is repeatedly stated as "that they may know that I am YHWH." Like in the book of Hosea, the need for the knowledge of God is what Ezekiel proclaims. Consequently, profaning the holy name of YHWH Ezekiel considers to be the most awful sin (Ezek. 20:8–13). Yet unlike earlier generations, the prophet holds each individual responsible within community (Ezek. 18:1–4).

> The word of the LORD came to me: What do you mean by repeating this proverb concerning the land of Israel, "The parents have eaten sour grapes, and the children's teeth are set on edge"? As I live, says the Lord GOD, this proverb shall no more be used by you in Israel. Know that all lives are mine; the life of

the parent as well as the life of the child is mine: it is only the person who sins that shall die.

So from the time of the Exile, the concept of corporate responsibility begins to weaken, replaced by an emphasis on individual accountability. Having experienced dispersion, the prophet Ezekiel offers responses both in terms of ethics and theology. After the destruction there will be restoration and renewal (Ezek. 36:22–32), a resurrection of the nation (Ezek. 37:1–14). Despite later interpretations, the emphasis is on renewal of the nation; it is not a prediction of individual resurrection, of an afterlife, but of a restoration of the people, guided by YHWH, the good shepherd (Ezek. 34:1–16). Indeed, there is hope for a people in exile!

The Unnamed Prophet of the Exile: Second Isaiah

Another prophet who gives comfort and vision to a defeated people is the unnamed prophet of the Exile known as Second Isaiah or Deutero-Isaiah (Isa. 40–55). Near the end of the exilic period (550–540 BCE), the prophet does not give us any information about who he or she is, with no biographical details intruding on her or his message. In rather lengthy poems we hear the voice of a poet delivering oracles of salvation; they are not messages of judgment and doom but ones of hope and reassurance. We encounter a treasure trove of female imagery, yet there is no way to prove that Deutero-Isaiah was a woman.

> For a long time I have held my peace, I have kept still and restrained; now I will cry out like a woman

in labor, I will gasp and pant. (Isa. 42:14; see also
45:9–10)

Listen to me, O house of Jacob, all the remnant of
the house of Israel, who have been borne by me from
your birth, carried from the womb (Isa. 46:3–4; see
also Isa. 49:14–15; 66:12–13)

The prophecies of the poet-prophet of the Exile open
with words of comfort:

> Comfort, O comfort my people, says your God.
> Speak tenderly to Jerusalem,
> and cry to her
> that she has served her term,
> that her penalty is paid,
> that she has received from the LORD's hand
> double for all her sins. (Isa. 40:1–2).

Now the prophet speaks of *my* people and not *this* people,
as in Isaiah 6. The distance has been removed. Indeed,
YHWH is said to evoke tenderness, promising forgiveness,
calling the Exile double punishment. As we hear these
verses read in synagogues and churches, keep in mind the
context for this word of comfort: it is not comfort for those
already well off, but for those who have suffered too much.
Isaiah of the Exile continues:

> A voice cries out:
> "In the wilderness prepare the way of the LORD,
> make straight in the desert a highway for our God.
> Every valley shall be lifted up,
> and every mountain and hill be made low;

the uneven ground shall become level,
and the rough places a plain.
Then the glory of the LORD shall be revealed,
and all people shall see it together,
for the mouth of the LORD has spoken."

(Isa. 40:3–5)

Recalling Israel's journey from Egypt to Sinai to Canaan
to Babylon with God, the prophet invokes the in-between
time in the *midbar*, promising reversals of realities through
the weight of God's presence (*kabod*, the Hebrew word
often translated as "glory," literally means "heaviness") and
by divine fiat.

A voice says, "Cry out!"
And I said, "What shall I cry?"
All people are grass,
their constancy is like the flower of the field.
The grass withers, the flower fades,
when the breath of the LORD blows upon it;
surely the people are grass.
The grass withers, the flower fades;
but the word of our God will stand forever.

(Isa. 40:6–8)

The reversals continue and remind the people of their humanity, juxtaposing it to the eternal word of God. An
eschatological promise of YHWH's beneficial presence as a
shepherd of the people concludes the exilic poet/prophet's
opening poem:

Get you up to a high mountain,
O Zion, herald of good tidings;

lift up your voice with strength,
O Jerusalem, herald of good tidings,
lift it up, do not fear;
say to the cities of Judah,
"Here is your God!"
See, the Lord GOD comes with might,
and his arm rules for him;
his reward is with him,
and his recompense before him.
He will feed his flock like a shepherd;
he will gather the lambs in his arms,
and carry them in his bosom,
and gently lead the mother sheep.

(Isa. 40:9–11)

Isaiah of the Exile prophesies the imminent deliverance of Israel from exile, grounding all promises in the claim that YHWH is the one God, the creator of the ends of the earth: "I am the first and I am the last; besides me there is no god" (Isa. 44:6; see also Isa. 41:4; 43:10; 44:8; 45:5–7, 14, 18, 22; 48:12). Here we find the first biblical statement of monotheism. Prior to that point, the Scriptures held various views of monolatry, the worship of one god without denying the existence of other gods. Indeed, we witnessed YHWH competing with the gods of Canaan and Mesopotamia. Now, in the Exile, the claim of monotheism gives hope as it challenges theological perspectives.

It is YHWH as creator and liberator, the God of the covenant who is calling on Israel, the servant to bring change.

Thus says God, the LORD,
who created the heavens and stretched them out,
who spread out the earth and what comes from it,
who gives breath to the people upon it
and spirit to those who walk in it:
I am the LORD, I have called you in righteousness,
I have taken you by the hand and kept you;
I have given you as a covenant to the people,
a light to the nations,
to open the eyes that are blind,
to bring out the prisoners from the dungeon,
from the prison those who sit in darkness.
I am the LORD/YHWH, that is my name;
my glory I give to no other,
nor my praise to idols.
See the former things have come to pass,
and new things I now declare;
before they spring forth, I tell you of them.

(Isa. 42:5–9)

Will the people "get it" this time? The prospects are slim, so YHWH promises divine forgiveness (43:25). Israel is promised a New Exodus (43:14–15). Liberation from Babylonian captivity will come through King Cyrus of Persia, who in Isaiah 45:1 is called the anointed, the messiah.

Much of the language and imagery of Isaiah 40–55 is familiar to many Christians from lectionary readings during both Advent and Lent, and none more so than the four Isaianic poems known as the "Servant Songs" (Isa. 42:1–4; 49:1–6; 50:4–9; 52:13–53:12), because the figure of the servant has been reinterpreted in Christian traditions in light of the passion narratives in the gospels of the Second Testament. Since such deeply ingrained convictions have hindered many readers from understanding these exilic poems in their own context, it is important to look closely at what we can learn about the servant in Isaiah.

The first task of the servant is to bring justice to the nations and coastlands beyond exiled Yehud.

> Here is my servant, whom I uphold,
> my chosen, in whom my soul delights;
> I have put my spirit upon him;
> he will bring forth justice to the nations.
> He will not cry or lift up his voice,
> or make it heard in the street;
> a bruised reed he will not break,
> and a dimly burning wick he will not quench;
> he will faithfully bring forth justice.
> He will not grow faint or be crushed
> until he has established justice in the earth;
> and the coastlands wait for his teaching.
> (Isa. 42:1–4)

The servant, who is created from the womb, brought forth by God, the midwife, is identified as Israel, who is to be a light to the nations.

> Listen to me, O coastlands,
> pay attention, you peoples from far away!
> The LORD called me before I was born,
> while I was in my mother's womb he named me.

He made my mouth like a sharp sword,
in the shadow of his hand he hid me;
he made me a polished arrow,
in his quiver he hid me away.
And he said to me, "You are my servant, Israel,
in whom I will be glorified."
But I said, "I have labored in vain,
I have spent my strength for nothing and vanity;
yet surely my cause is with the LORD,
and my reward with my God.
And now the LORD says,
who formed me in the womb to be his servant,
to bring Jacob back to him,
and that Israel might be gathered to him,
for I am honored in the sight of the LORD,
and my God has become my strength —
he says,
"It is too light a thing that you should be my servant
to raise up the tribes of Jacob
and to restore the survivors of Israel;
I will give you as a light to the nations,
that my salvation may reach to the end of the earth."

(Isa. 49:1–6)

As a teacher, the servant is to comfort the weary:

The Lord GOD has given me the tongue of a teacher,
that I may know how to sustain the weary with a word.
Morning by morning he wakens — wakens my ear
to listen as those who are taught.
The Lord GOD has opened my ear,
and I was not rebellious,

I did not turn backward.
I gave my back to those who struck me,
and my cheeks to those who pulled out the beard;
I did not hide my face from insult and spitting.

(Isa. 50:4–6)

Suffering is part of the servant's reality, suffering of one's own as well as vicarious suffering according to the will of God (Isa. 52:13–53:12).

Surely he has borne our infirmities
and carried our diseases;
yet we accounted him stricken,
struck down by God, and afflicted.
But he was wounded for our transgressions,
crushed for our iniquities;
upon him was the punishment that made us whole,
and by his bruises we are healed. (Isa. 53:4–5)

Attempts at identifying the servant have been endless. Individual identifications have included historical figures from Moses to Job in the First Testament, including the poet-prophet of Isaiah 40–55 herself- or himself. Christians in later centuries have substituted Jesus of Nazareth for the servant, helped by passages in the Gospels of Matthew and John referencing the book of Isaiah. The identification of Israel as the servant in the text has pointed to a collective interpretation that may refer either to the exiled Israel of the sixth century BCE, an ideal Israel of the future, or a remnant within Israel. Considering the fact that the servant is also mentioned throughout other chapters in Deutero-Isaiah (Isa. 41–45; 48) and not only in the four poems considered the servant songs, more doubts have been raised as to the identification of an individual. In Isaiah 41:8–10; 43:10; 44:1–2, 21–22 the servant is identified as Israel/Jacob collectively. Further, Israel/Jacob shares characteristics with Zion/Jerusalem in the way they are portrayed, both complaining about their treatment by YHWH's hand and both being promised vindication, among other similarities in themes and motifs.[4]

Transformed from suffering to something new to be celebrated, Israel hears the prophecies of Isaiah of the Exile, which began with calling for comfort for a distraught and exhausted people, and come to a close with an invitation to a banquet in the restored Zion (Isa. 55). A glorious vision after a wrenching war — theological questions notwithstanding.

Study Questions

1. What have you learned about the Exile?

2. What theological responses to the experience of Exile have emerged?

3. How do you understand the prophecies of Ezekiel?

4. Who was Ezekiel the prophet?

5. What characterizes the prophecies of the voice known as Second Isaiah?

6. How would you describe the servant figure in Isa. 40–55?

7. What elements of Isa. 1–39 do you hear echoed in Isa. 40–55?

Further Reading

Brueggemann, Walter. *Hopeful Imagination: Prophetic Voices in Exile*. Philadelphia: Fortress Press, 1986.

Smith-Christopher, Daniel L. *A Biblical Theology of Exile*. Overtures to Biblical Theology. Minneapolis: Fortress Press, 2002, chapters 1–4.

Notes

1. James A. Sanders, *From Sacred Story to Sacred Text* (Philadelphia: Fortress Press, 1987).

2. Daniel L. Smith-Christopher, *A Biblical Theology of Exile*, Overtures to Biblical Theology (Minneapolis: Fortress Press, 2002), 27–73.

3. Ellen F. Davis, *Swallowing the Scroll: Textuality and the Dynamics of Discourse in Ezekiel's Prophecy*, JSOT Supplement 78, Bible and Literature Series 21 (Sheffield: Almond Press, 1989).

4. Patricia Tull Willey, *"Remember the Former Things": The Recollection of Previous Texts in Second Isaiah* (Atlanta: Scholars Press, 1997).

Chapter Eight

Responses to Exile

Liturgical and Wisdom Texts

Read: Isaiah 56–66; selected Psalms (e.g., 1, 8, 22, 43, 44, 85, 104, 137, 139, 150); Lamentations; Job; reread Genesis 1.

In 539 BCE the Babylonian Empire comes to an end. The Persians take over and conquer all the land to the borders of Egypt. King Cyrus comes to power, and in 538 he issues a decree concerning the Jews (official proclamation in Aramaic Ezra 6:3–5; a Hebrew version is found in Ezra 1:2–4). This is when the exilic period officially ends. The Jewish people are allowed to go back to their homeland, and the return begins under the leadership of Sheshbazzar. But not all the people went.

We do not know the ratio between the numbers of those who returned and those who remained in Babylon. But it is clear that a significant number of Jews decided to stay there rather than relocate, and that from now on the history of Yehud/Israel had at least two focal points: the "mother" country and the Diaspora. The following decades show that there was an intimate relationship between the two, indeed that the Jews living in the Diaspora felt a degree of responsibility for conditions in the mother country and that they exercised an important influence.

An archive of clay tablets from the second half of the fifth century BCE found in the Babylonian mercantile city of Nippur gives us a glimpse into the life of the Jewish Diaspora. It contains the business records of the banking house of Murashu. Here, among the names of the multinational clientele, there are also numerous Jewish names, the bearers of which were obviously intensively occupied in the trading and commercial life of their locality; in some cases they also occupied leading positions in commerce or public life.[1] The names show that the bearers kept their Jewish identity, which is expressed, e.g., in the preservation of names with the element *yahu* or *yaw* (=YHWH).

The biblical texts give us no direct information about the social and economic situation in Yehud, only hints (e.g., Isa. 56–66). So we do not discover the effect of the change in the ownership of property after the deportation and what arrangements were made between those who returned and those who remained in the country. It was most likely a relatively small group of families that decided to return to desolation, to rebuild the temple as a continuation of the line of David. They went back with words of Ezekiel and Isaiah of the Exile ringing in their ears; they met despair and frustration; there was no mighty reversal in the cosmos. "It was a day of small things" (Zech. 4:10); the land lay in ruins; crops were failing; and worship practices had deteriorated.

In 515 BCE the temple is rededicated, but there is no real rejoicing. The whole thing is a disappointment; the heavens and the earth are not turned upside down after all. The people weep, remembering Solomon's temple. The prophet Haggai, who was active around 520 BCE during the time of Persian king Darius (522–486 BCE), describes the new one as a little shack by comparison (Hag. 1:2–11). Such is the beginning of the so-called Second Temple period.

The books of Ezra and Nehemiah describe these times further. Nehemiah (ca. 440 BCE), with the permission of Xerxes to rebuild the fortification of Jerusalem, is appointed governor of Yehud. His mission is one of getting the people to give to the temple, observe the sabbath, and end inter-marriages. Ezra (ca. 428 BCE), a scribe, whose religious mission is to enforce the law, stresses allegiance to YHWH as being dependent on life according to the Torah and introduces regular public Torah readings.

By the fifth century BCE prophecy has faded, as prophecy ceases to speak to the people in postexilic times.[2] Inconsistencies between experience and expectation, promises and the lack of their realization created cognitive dissonances. Avoidance, exclusionary group behaviors, or reframing the experience were the strategies then (as they are today) to lessen the tensions. When something is too hard to face, people tend to avoid it, not deal with it. When something is too hard to face, people often resort to huddling down with those closest and most comfortable, stopping the harder work of connecting to the different and new. When a situation gets worse, old and new hostilities toward the "other" (re)emerge. Further, when something is too hard to face, people try to find explanations of why it happened and who is to blame. Our ancestors did it; the people of Yehud did it; and we do it, too. Realizing that prophecy had put far too great a burden on historical and political developments to fulfill spiritual needs and answer theological questions, the people turned to different modes of living their theological worldviews.

The void created by failing prophecy is filled by apocalypticism, which releases history from the burden of God's revelation by promising a future for the elect in a time beyond time (Isa. 24–27; Zech. 12–14; Daniel), and wisdom, which instead gives authority to personal experience and timeless practical knowledge (Proverbs, Job, Ecclesiastes/Qoheleth).

The Hebrew word for wisdom is *hokmah,* meaning wisdom as intelligence, skill, and superior mental ability. It is a quest for understanding on the level of nature; to master things on a juridical level; to function in human relationships within society; and, on a theological level, wisdom engages the relationship between the human and the divine.[3]

In the Hebrew Bible there are different types of wisdom: prudential wisdom literature (e.g., Proverbs) and reflective wisdom literature (e.g., Job; Qoheleth/Ecclesiastes). Not unique to Israel, wisdom traditions are an Ancient Near Eastern phenomenon (Egypt; Mesopotamia). However, Israel's tradition has a distinct twist, as stated in the book of Proverbs: "... the fear of YHWH is the beginning of wisdom" (Prov. 1:1–7).

For the people of Yehud/Israel, the experience of exile and return requires new meaning making. As we have seen earlier, there is the impulse to make sense of what has happened, as we see in the search for reasons in history that the Deuteronomistic historians undertake in the exilic redaction of the Deuteronomistic History, where unconditional covenants get subordinated to conditional covenants, and the Exile is understood as punishment for past disobedience (see chapters 4 and 7 above).

Another powerful response to exile is lament, the mourning of things lost. There is a whole book in the Hebrew Bible dedicated to doing exactly that, the book of Lamentations. And there are psalms of lament; Ps 137 stands out in mentioning the Babylonian experience explicitly. All cry out to YHWH asking for relief. Among the psalms, there are also psalms of wisdom.

The Book of Psalms

The Psalter is probably the best-known book of the Bible in the Jewish as well as in the Christian tradition, since the psalms are still prayed and sung in our liturgies. The English title "Psalms" is derived from the Greek *psalmoi* "songs of praise."

Traditionally it is David who is associated with the psalms, and there are many superscriptions attributing psalms to him, as well as the final line in Psalm 72: "the *tefillot*, the prayers of David have ended." The psalms do come, however, from various periods within the history of Israel-Judah. Some of these are attributions in honor of David, not claiming Davidic authorship.

Modeled after Torah, the Psalter divides into five books (Pss. 3–41; 42–72; 73–89; 90–106; 107–150), each ending in a doxology or hymn of praise (41:14; 72:18f; 89:53; 106:48; and 150). It contains evidence of earlier collections. For a long time considered the prayer book of the Second Temple, the psalms were also very popular at

Qumran (a psalms scroll from Cave 11 contains fragments of at least 115 psalms in an altogether different sequence), and they are still popular today. One reason for the continued use of the psalms is the fact that they are open-ended. The laments are future oriented, ending with a vow of praise in anticipation. In their language of relationality ("I-Thou"), in their quality of existential understanding of the human condition, the psalms have had a timeless quality. Recent scholarship, while recognizing that psalms may well have arisen out of and for the sake of liturgical practice, contends that the Psalter itself is now independent of the cult and stands as a source of meditation on Torah. They now are understood to have *instructional* character.

Form critics have identified basic forms/genres of psalms:

1. hymns, e.g., 8, 19, 29; includes Songs of Zion: 46, 48, 76, 84, 87, 122;

2. psalms of YHWH's enthronement, e.g., 47, 93, 97, 99;

3. royal psalms, e.g., 2, 18, 20, 72;

4. laments: of community, e.g., 44, 74, 79, 80, 83; of individual, e.g., 22, 35, 42–43, 86;

5. thanksgivings, e.g., 67, 92, 138;

6. wisdom psalms, e.g., 1, 37, 49, 73, 111, 112, 127, 128, 133; and

7. mixed types.[4]

The psalms arose out of the midst of Israel's life in the presence of God, responding to good times and bad, providing words for the celebrations of the community, and offering guidance and reflection on the opportunities and problems of life. The Psalter itself teaches that we must place our trust in God and not in the monarchy (the governing body). In its canonical form as a response to the experiences of exile, the book of Psalms offers guidance away from unquestioning reliance on leaders to a recommitment to the covenant between God and the people.

The Book of Job

Yet another response to the exilic experience is the reframing of theological worldviews. There is the struggle to make sense of what happened within the tried and true framework of beliefs, and the recognition of the need for a different understanding of faith and faithfulness that is found within Wisdom, in terms of the exilic experience, especially the book of Job.

Considered exilic or postexilic, the book of Job is one whose topic is often considered the question of evil or the question of theodicy. Unlike the orthodox Deuteronomistic or proverbial understandings of a theology of retribution, which consider suffering a result of wrongdoing and therefore the Exile as a result of Israel's sin, the book of Job offers another perspective — anti-wisdom wisdom, if you will.

The book is structured as a narrated prologue and a narrated epilogue, with poetic dialogue in between. In the prologue the *satan* ("Satan" is not a personal name or a title) is sent by God to test Job. Job passes the first test, yet the second test makes him sick (Job 1–2). Sitting on a dung heap, Job receives three of his friends who come to visit and offer their theological explanations in three cycles of speeches (Job 3–14; 15–21; 22–27), concluding with a hymn to wisdom (Job 28). Job eventually responds, dismissing their advice (Job 29–31). A fourth friend tries to do better, but to no avail (Job 32–37). Finally, God speaks (Job 38–42), and Job replies on two occasions. The epilogue connects back to the narrative of the prologue (Job 42:7–17).

The book of Job has raised many questions and invited dramatization through the ages. The prose frame, perhaps an ancient folktale — the name "Job" is a historical name (see Ezek. 14:13–23) — is an Edomite tale that at one point becomes a Hebrew story and in time a framework for the book. Yet there is a tension between prose and poetry, though it might very well be that without the prose we wouldn't have the dialogue. In the folktale we see a patient Job ("God gives and God takes away; blessed be the name of God"); in the dialogue Job is anything but patient. In the folktale we see an obedient Job; in the dialogue Job is blasphemous. In the folktale we see Job as a model of religiosity who blesses; in the dialogue Job is a model of doubting, who rebels and curses. In the folktale we see a Job who represents orthodoxy according to the doctrine of retribution; in the dialogue Job represents heresy, claiming that the doctrine of retribution does not work in his case.

The narrative frame sets up an exemplary test case: a just person has been struck down by misfortune. It draws us in; we all know this experience. Then it moves from the typical to a deeper level. Enter the dialogue: from talking *about* suffering from the *outside* (talking about Job), the dialogue moves to talking about suffering from *within* (Job talking).

In both Job is at the center — but differently; in both Job's suffering is tied to the issue of integrity, the issue of perfection: Hebrew *tam* (wholeness, uprightness, completeness). This is Job; Job is morally perfect (thus allowing for a perfect test). So we encounter here a trial *occasioned* by suffering *not caused* by it, a trial of faith in which Job demands that his integrity be vindicated, and this very demand becomes his problem. To understand the book we must accept the premise of Job's uprightness at face value. Enter the friends: they have the thankless role of characterizing conventional wisdom. Without these friends Job could have disintegrated. Unable to bear suffering alone, though he is "alone," in arguing he gains some freedom to think differently. The speeches appear endless, offering a narrow moral vision of the world with little compassion.

The speeches of God shift the direction of the dialogue with question after question and none having to do with Job's situation. Job offers to capitulate (Job 40:2); yet God comes back. When God gets through this time, Job understands and offers a confession, "Therefore I recant and change my mind about dust and ashes" (Job 42:6), about the human condition; about who I am and about who you are.[5]

In the end many questions are not solved, but they have become irrelevant in the face of transformation. Job changed his mind about looking at life by absolutizing a vision of retributive theology, of moralistic clichés. Indeed, reframing leads to liberation.

The Priestly Creation Story

The Priestly writers provide another way of reframing, taking the people back to creation and the covenant with Noah, and eventually laying out rules and regulations to prevent another experience like the Exile. The Priestly School reconfigures its worldview with another story of creation, quite different from the chaos of the contemporary state of the world.

Genesis 1:1–2:4a stands over against the official Akkadian creation myth *Enuma Elish*, "when on high the heaven had not been named" (Tablet I.1), as well as the creation myth of Babylon, which portrays a world of insecurity and violence where the gods fight each other and humans are made to serve them. Into that context, Genesis 1 offers a creation myth ordering the world in seven days. On the first three days God creates the universe, and on the last three populates it:[6]

first day	*fourth day*
light is separated from darkness (1:3–5)	the greater and lesser lights separate day and night (1:14–19)
second day	*fifth day*
the firmament separates the waters (1:6–8)	water and air animals appear (1:20–23)
third day	*sixth day*
the earth appears the earth puts forth vegetation (1:9–13)	land animals appear humankind is made (1:24–30)

Throughout, specific words, phrases, and themes recur to unite the entire cosmos in harmony. The word *ṭov* "good" appears seven times: Genesis 1:4, 10, 12, 18, 21, 25, 31, and the seventh climactic one, "very good."

> In the beginning when God created/when God began to create the heavens and the earth, the earth was a formless void and darkness covered the face of the deep, while a wind/spirit from God swept over the face of the waters. Then God said, "Let there be light"; and there was light. And God saw that the light was good; and God separated the light from the darkness. God called the light Day, and the darkness he called Night. And there was evening and there was morning, the first day. (Gen. 1:1–5)

And so it opens: "In the beginning God" or "when God began" — the consonants of the Hebrew word allow for either reading — to create the heavens and the earth there was not evil, but only chaos, void, emptiness, until the words of God "let there be" become creative action, "and there was" or "God made."

Further, God assigns responsibility to the earth for participating in the creative process (Gen. 1:11–12). God blesses the birds and the fish, wild animals, domestic animals, and their blessing is responsibility in creation. The subsequent creation of humans differs both in length and in description:

> Then God said, "Let us make humankind in our image, according to our likeness; and let them have dominion over the fish of the sea, and over the birds of the air, and over the cattle, and over all the wild animals of

the earth, and over every creeping thing that creeps upon the earth." So God created humankind in his image, in the image of God he created them; male and female he created them. (Gen. 1:26–27)

Humans are created in the image and after the likeness of God, male and female, as God's representatives on the earth. The image of God "male *and* female" calls for a gender inclusive portrayal of God the Creator. Humans, like the earth, are given responsibility by being given power over the animals (Gen. 1:28–31). The biblical text calls this power "dominion," a fateful word because it has become confused with domination over the earth and its creatures, and by extension a permission to exploit either. Contrary to the history of its interpretation, the Priestly creation story proclaims the pivotal human task as the responsibility to preserve the goodness of creation.

God saw everything that he had made, and indeed, it was very good. (Gen. 1:31)

After surveying the state of creation, God rests on the seventh day (Gen. 2:1–3). The day is made holy, *qadosh*, set apart. Indeed, God's rest completes the work of creation. Thus the sabbath becomes a foundational element of the vision of faithful living after the Exile.

Whether lamenting the experienced suffering or transcending it through new awareness, whether explaining the cause of destruction or juxtaposing it with a vision of an orderly creation, biblical responses to the Exile offer us insights as we grow in our own interpretations of the Hebrew Scriptures.

Study Questions

1. How do you understand the demise of biblical prophecy?

2. What have you learned about biblical developments filling the gap left by prophecy?

3. What are the main tenets of biblical wisdom?

4. What are the characteristics of biblical apocalypticism?

5. How do you understand the book of Job?

6. What are some of the elements of the Priestly creation account?

7. Comparing and contrasting various biblical responses to the experience of Exile, what theological insights emerge?

Further Reading

Bergant, Dianne. *Israel's Wisdom Literature: A Liberation-Critical Reading*. Minneapolis: Fortress Press, 1997.

Janzen, Gerald J. *Job*. Interpretation, a Bible Commentary for Teaching and Preaching. Atlanta: John Knox Press, 1985.

Smith-Christopher, Daniel L. *A Biblical Theology of Exile*. Overtures to Biblical Theology. Minneapolis: Fortress Press, 2002, chapters 5–8.

Notes

1. Michael Coogan, "Life in the Diaspora: Jews at Nippur in the Fifth Century BC," *Biblical Archaeologist* 37 (1974): 6–12.

2. Robert P. Carroll, *When Prophecy Failed: Cognitive Dissonance in the Prophetic Traditions of the Old Testament* (Minneapolis: Seabury Press, 1979; London: XPress Reprints, 1996).

3. Gerhard von Rad, *Wisdom in Israel* (Nashville: Abingdon Press, 1972; orig. 1970).

4. Hermann Gunkel, *The Psalms: A Form-Critical Introduction* (Philadelphia: Fortress Press, 1967; orig. 1922).

5. Based on Gerald Janzen's reading in his commentary, *Job*, Interpretation, a Bible Commentary for Teaching and Preaching (Atlanta: John Knox Press, 1985).

6. Based on Phyllis Trible, *God and the Rhetoric of Sexuality*, Overtures to Biblical Theology (Philadelphia: Fortress Press, 1978), 12–21.

Tables

Chronology of the Composition of the First Testament/Hebrew Bible

As we have seen throughout this guidebook, the date of composition of a biblical book does not necessarily coincide with the date of its written sources. Indeed, for the most part, the final edition of the majority of books in the First Testament/Hebrew Bible is dated much later, many during the Babylonian exile (586–538 BCE) or after. The dates given below refer to the assumed times of the original composition rather than of the final editing. Further, hypothetical written sources appear in brackets.

tenth century BCE	[Yahwist (J) (ca. 950)]
ninth century BCE	[Elohist (E) (ca. 850)]
eighth century BCE	Amos (ca. 760–750)
	Hosea (ca. 750–725)
	Isaiah 1–39 (742–701)
	Micah (725–701)
	Ruth?
seventh century BCE	[J + E (ca. 700)]
	Joshua–Kings (ca. 680)
	[D (ca. 630)]
	Zephaniah (640–609)

seventh century BCE	Nahum (shortly before 612)
	Jeremiah (626–587)
	Habakkuk (609–598)
sixth century BCE	Ezekiel (593–586)
	Obadiah (shortly after 586)
	Lamentations?
	Isaiah 40–55 (ca. 550)
	[P + JE + D (ca. 550)]
	Haggai (ca. 520)
	Zechariah 1–8 (520–518)
fifth century BCE	Job?
	Jonah?
	Joel?
	Zechariah 9–14 (ca. 450?)
	Ezra-Nehemiah (458–430)
	Malachi (ca. 445)
	Ruth?
fourth century BCE	Qoheleth/Ecclesiastes
	Chronicles
	Esther
	Song of Songs?
second century BCE	Daniel

The book of Psalms contains psalms dating from the ninth to the fourth centuries; the book of Proverbs also collects sayings from various periods.

Chronology of Rulers in the Ancient Near East until ca. 500 BCE

Dates in the following table indicate the approximate reign of rulers, not the length of their lives. Reconstructions from biblical records alone do not allow for a coherent picture. Scholars have arrived at approximations such as the one here from comparing historical and archaeological records with the biblical chronologies. All dates are BCE (Before the Common Era). Further, dates and events that do not have extrabiblical corroboration are put in brackets.

Chronology of Rulers in the Ancient Near East until ca. 500 BCE

Canaan	*Syria*	*Egypt*
	Hittite rulers (ca. 1550–1200)	Rameses II (1279–1213)
		Merneptah (1213–1203)
[Exodus of		
Hebrews from Egypt]		
Israelite Judges ca. 1150–1020]		
Israel		
Saul (1020–1000)		
David (1000–965)		
Solomon (968–922)		

Judah	*Israel*
	Jeroboam I (922–901)
Rehoboam (922–915)	
Abijam (915–913)	
Asa (913–873)	Nadab (901–900)
	Baasha (900–877)
	Elah (877–876)
	Zimri (876)
Jehoshaphat (873–849)	Omri (876–869)
	Ahab (869–850)
	Ahaziah (850)
	Jehoram (849–843/842)
Jehoram (849–843/842)	
Ahaziah (843/842)	
Queen Athaliah (843/842–837)	

Judah	Israel	Assyria	Persia
Jehoash (837–800)	Jehu (843/842–815)	*Assyria*	
Amaziah (800–783)	Jehoahaz (815–802)	Tiglath-pileser III (745–727)	
Uzziah (783–742)	Joash (802–786)		
	Jeroboam II (786–746)		
Jotham (742–735)	Zechariah (746–745)		
	Shallum (745–737)	Shalmanezer V (727–722)	
	Menahem (745–737)	Sargon II (722–705)	
	Pekahiah (737–736)	Sennacherib (705–681)	
	Pekah (736–732)		
	Hoshea (732–724)		
	Fall of Samaria (722)		
Hezekiah (715–687)			
Assyrian invasion (701)			
Manasseh (687–642)			
Ammon (642–640)			
Josiah (640–609)			
Jehoahaz/Shallum (609)			
Jehoakim (609–598)			
Jehoiachin (598/597)			
First Babylonian Siege of Jerusalem and First Deportation (597)			
Zedekiah (597–587/586)			
Babylonian Seizure of Jerusalem and Second Deportation (586)			
			Persia
			Cyrus II (559–530)
			Cambyses (530–522)
			Darius I (522–486)
Jews return from Babylon (538)			
Reconstruction of the temple (520–515)